Pick a Card,
Any Card

THE AUTHOR

*Harry Baron was President of The Magic Club International,
an Associate of The Inner Magic Circle, member of
The International Brotherhood of Magicians,
Mephisto Magic Club and
numerous other Magical Organisations.*

Other books by Harry Baron

MAGIC FOR BEGINNERS
MY BEST CARD TRICK
MY BEST CLOSE-UP TRICK
CLOSE UP MAGIC FOR BEGINNERS

How to Order:

Single copies may be ordered from Prima Publishing, P.O. Box
1260BK, Rocklin, CA 95677; telephone (916) 632-4400. Quantity
discounts are also available. On your letterhead, include information
concerning the intended use of the books and the number of books you
wish to purchase.

Information for the Receiver

ur friend Trent has requested the book(s) above for
u from another member at PaperBackSwap. This
ok was requested by Trent and was mailed to you by
ren LeHotay. Please contact Trent when you receive
s so the book can be marked in our system as
ceived. If you are not a member of PaperBackSwap,
k Trent about the great features on the site. Join us
ay and become a member of the best online book
b in America!

ssage From Trent:

Pick a Card, Any Card

Card Tricks
for
Beginners

HARRY BARON

Illustrations posed by Jerry Sadowitz

Prima Publishing
P.O. Box 1260 BK
Rocklin, CA 95677
(916) 632-4400

First published in Great Britain by Breese Books Limited,
164 Kensington Park Road, London W11 2ER

Cover design by Lindy Dunlavey, The Dunlavey Studio
Cover illustration by Jeff Bane

Library of Congress Cataloging-in-Publication Data
Baron, Harry, 1919-
    [Card tricks for beginners]
    Pick a card, any card : card tricks for beginners / Harry Baron.
        p.   cm.
    Originally published as: Card tricks for beginners.
    ISBN 1-55958-493-9
    1. Card tricks.   I. Title.
GV1549.B32   1994
795.4'38—dc20   94-6125
                                                    CIP

95 96 97 AA 10 9 8 7 6 5 4 3

Printed in the United States of America

Contents

Foreword

by JOE STUTHARD

*H*ARRY BARON has written a remarkable book – I have read many books on conjuring, and card magic in particular, but on reading this manuscript I have discovered many fine card tricks some of which I have already used in my television appearances.

This book on card tricks is not designed for the professional although the seasoned performers will gain much from it; rather it is intended for the many thousands of magical enthusiasts to be found in every civilized country. In my travels throughout the world I have had the privilege of being the guest of Magic Clubs in various countries and have noted the increasing interest in this fascinating hobby.

Harry Baron, whose job it was to invent, make and sell magic, was well known in the world of magic, and in these pages has unstintingly passed on the vital and valuable information about card tricks which will be of unsurpassing benefit to all those who read it. This 'know how' has been amassed over the years — I only wish I could have had this book in my hands many years ago, when I first became interested.

Publisher's Note

Sadly Harry Baron died early in 1991 while this revised edition of his work was being prepared. He was a wonderful magician and most popular with his friends and colleagues in and out of the magic world. He collapsed whilst he was performing at a charity function and died not long after. He was a kind and gentle man always prepared to assist and help others improve their magic.

Introduction

*T*HE popularity of card tricks never seems to falter, probably it is due to the basic simplicity of the apparatus – just a pack of cards. Of course card tricks have an appeal to all age groups. Many enthusiasts even do card tricks merely to amuse themselves and spend hours working out clever effects and problems with cards.

Basically however, magic is a visual art, and it is usually to entertain others that we perform tricks, and of course the audience is also an important factor in the successful presentation of a good effect. Part of the joy of performing magic tricks is the sensation arising from the ability to entertain. That does not mean that you must always amuse them, or always mystify them, but whenever you perform, you must at least always endeavour to *entertain* them.

The tricks described throughout this book have been selected because of their impact on the audience; they are, in the main, fairly easy to perform. This will leave ample opportunity for the reader to pay greater attention to their presentation, using showmanship to make the tricks more interesting, and of course more entertaining.

But as with all things worthwhile, there are basic principles to master. To drive a car one must become familiar with the gears; so with the successful performance of card tricks, the beginner must learn a few of what we term 'sleights'. They are the 'gears' we use to execute the tricks, the mechanics in fact. On a car they are out of sight and the good driver allows them to perform their function easily and noiselessly. So with the sleights – the audience ought not to be aware of their existence. Strive to use them effortlessly without thinking about them.

If you will allow the analogy a little further, this book is like our car, possessing no more gears than is necessary. The sleights you will learn are sufficient for every trick described, but they will also take you along many further 'miles' of practical performances doing tricks with cards and entertaining people.

I am indebted to many magicians who have made this work possible – those known and unknown, who have brought forth, improved on and added to the many ideas that go to making up a card trick. My own task has been to collate this material, perhaps adding a little here and there in order to present to the reader a compact collection of card magic, which is what you will find between these covers.

H. B.

CHAPTER ONE

Tricks with a Borrowed Pack

*I*N every technical book the author finds it necessary to make use of certain words peculiar to his subject. Whilst an attempt has been made to keep the instructions contained in this book as simple as possible, the reader will nevertheless find various words which have their place only in conjuring jargon. But there is no need to worry, as suitable explanations will be provided to keep the beginner well informed.

It is to be hoped anyway, that the learner will soon embark into the realms of other magical literature, so at least he will be well-armed if he can assimilate some of the conjurer's terms.

I feel I must at this stage make a point about the frequent repetition of words throughout this book. It must be irksome to the reader, but the justification lies in stressing the importance of making myself clear. For instance, if a trick is being described and the words 'left-hand' are repeatedly used, I am sure the reader will feel more assisted and the purpose of this book will be more fulfilled if he is told just where and what his left hand should be doing at a given time.

However, it is time we got down to the real 'meat' in this book – how to do card tricks, so for the first chapter we will deal with tricks that can be performed using a borrowed pack. By having a few such tricks at your command you will never be at a loss when called upon to, 'Show us a few tricks'.

THE LONG-DISTANCE CARD TRICK

This is one of my favourite card tricks and no doubt it can become one of yours too, because you can actually perform it without ever handling or even seeing the cards.

You ask your friend to shuffle a pack of cards and fan them face towards him, then he selects any one of the spot cards. Incidentally your back can be turned or you can be in another room, or even conduct the proceedings over a telephone if you so desire.

Having decided on the card, he is told to take it out, square up the pack and turn it face down. His selected card is now placed on the top of the pack also face down. Now he is instructed to remove its value in cards from the bottom of the pack and place them on the top, for instance if he chose the Six of Diamonds, he simply takes six cards from the bottom and puts them on the top, above his card. He must do this silently so that no clue is given as to how many cards have been changed. He now deals the cards from the top of the pack one at a time on to the table, and calls out the names of each card as he does so. He continues with several cards and without changing the inflection in his voice so that this provides no clue either, goes right past his own card until you tell him to stop. Then you name his card.

The secret is very simple. All you have to do is wait until he begins to call the cards – ignore the first one, but begin silently to count one, two, three, as he calls out the remainder. Continue until he calls out a card which corresponds with the number you are silently counting. This will invariably be the card, but let him go on further for a card or two, then stop him and surprise him by announcing his card.

Try it for yourself and see how it works out. Sometimes, by accident, more than one card will correspond with your silent count, but if this happens take a chance and name the one you think. If he should say 'No', it will be the other.

Naturally the trick can be repeated, but it is inadvisable to perform it too many times at one sitting because an astute person may tumble to it.

THE FIVE-FINGER EXERCISE

When you begin to learn how to play the piano you are first taught the five-finger exercises; this trick can also be called the Piano Card Trick because it makes use of the five fingers held as if you really were playing the piano.

Sit opposite the spectator and ask him to put his hands on the table as if playing the piano. Now put two cards between the third and little finger of the left hand saying 'Here is a pair.' Next put another two cards between the third and second fingers, saying 'Here is another pair.' Then put two cards between the first and second fingers saying, 'And here is a pair as well.' Finally, place two cards between the forefinger and thumb, saying, 'And another pair here.' Repeat with the right hand but with the exception that only one card is put between the thumb and forefinger and at this point you say 'But this is an odd card.' The cards will appear as in Fig. 1.

Go over what you have done, saying 'This is a pair' and so on until you refer to the odd one which, you point out, is indeed an odd one.

Remove two cards from the spectator's left hand saying, 'Here's a pair,' and separate them, placing the two cards a few inches from each other on the table in front of his hand. Remove two more cards, separate them and put them on top of the others saying, 'Here is a pair.' Continue this until all the cards are used up from the left hand, and follow up in the same way with those from the right hand, until only one card remains. Hand this odd card to the spectator to place on top of any one of the

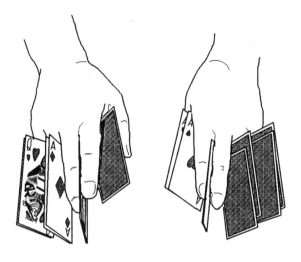

Fig. 1

piles. Tell him that you are going to cause this odd card to
pass from that pile to the other one. Give both piles a tap
saying that it has gone.

Pick up the original odd pile and separate two cards
saying, 'Here is a pair,' then another two saying,
'Another pair,' and so on. You will find that you have
four pairs – the odd card has vanished. Deal with the
other pile in a similar way, but here you will discover one
odd card, therefore proving the trick has worked.

The trick is really self-working. Follow it as already
described and surprise yourself.

Actually what happens is that the spectator holds four
pairs in the left hand and three pairs plus an odd one in
the right hand to start with. When they are divided into
two piles there will be seven cards in each but your
constant reiteration 'Here's a pair,' etc. will throw the
spectators off the track. When the odd card is added it
will actually make it an even pile, but always call two
cards a 'pair' when presenting the effect.

Phil Wye has suggested a variation – instead of handing the 'odd' card to the spectator, actually place it on the

pile yourself, do not show it, but mis-call it as a card which you know is at the bottom of the other pile.

Deal down both the piles to show that the card has passed, and show the 'named card' on top of the other pile.

SATAN REVERSE CARD TRICK

Any pack is used, and after being shuffled it is cut by a spectator into two piles. This person then selects one of the piles while the performer takes the other.

The performer turns his back and the spectator selects any card from his half pack, notes it and replaces it on top of his pile. The magician now turns round and places his half pack on top of the spectator's.

The spectator now takes the complete pack and holds it behind his back. He is instructed to remove the bottom card and insert it somewhere near the top of the pack, then to take the top card and insert it somewhere near the bottom. The now top card is reversed and placed somewhere near the centre and the pack brought into view once more. When the cards are spread, the reversed card is seen to be next to the selected card.

Method: After the pack has been shuffled, have the spectator cut it into two piles. He selects any one of these and you take the other, then turn your back. Instruct the spectator to remove any card he fancies, note it, and replace it on top of his pile. Meanwhile you take the opportunity to reverse the *bottom and second-from-top cards* in your pile. When you turn round, drop your pile on to his and give them to the spectator who places them behind his back. He is told to put the top card anywhere in the pack near the bottom, the bottom card near the top and the now top card reversed anywhere near the centre.

Naturally when the cards are spread there will be one card reversed (your original bottom reversed card) but he will take it to be the one he reversed and it will be *next* to his selected card.

MIRACLE CARD TRICK

This one is a positive stunner, and ideal to work if someone produces a pack of cards and asks you to perform an impromptu card trick. There is no need to touch the cards. Turn your back and instruct your friend first of all to shuffle the cards. Now ask him to think of any number between one and ten, and to count down to this number from the top of the face-down pack; he is to remember the card which lies at this position. He is then instructed silently to remove the number he thought of, in cards, from the bottom of the pack and place them on top.

For instance, if he thought of the number five, he first of all counts down to the fifth card and notes which card lies at that position. Now he removes five cards from the bottom of the pack and places them on top. The pack is squared up and handed to you behind your back.

After some deliberation you produce the pack, handing it back to your friend, and telling him that you have placed his card in its original position. He counts down to it and sure enough there is his actual selected card! How? Remember you did not know his original number, his selected card, or how many he counted from the bottom. It does seem like a miracle doesn't it?

When you receive the cards behind your back, you place the top card and *every other alternate card* up to ten on the bottom of the pack. That's all, because this now leaves the pack with your friend's selected card in its original position.

Here is an easy way to sort the alternate ten behind your back: try it with the cards in front of you first (Fig. 2). Hold the pack in the left hand as if for dealing, push

Fig. 2

the top card upwards so that its bottom half rests on the top half of the next card, now bring both of these down and level the top card with the third. Pick all three up and level the second card with the fourth, and so on until you have ten cards sticking out at the top. Strip all these out and put them on the bottom.

ACE AWAY

You show three Aces in a fan (Fig. 3), turning them face down they are placed in various parts of the pack. The spectator is now asked to name a colour, red or black. If he chooses red, say that you will cause the Red Ace (the Ace of Diamonds) to leave the pack and pass into your pocket. He holds the pack tightly but despite this you reach into your pocket and extract the Ace. Of course the pack can be thoroughly examined; only the three Aces are there.

If the black Aces are selected, you merely state that it leaves you with the Ace of Diamonds, which you will

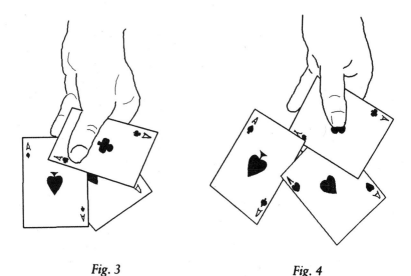

Fig. 3   *Fig. 4*

cause to pass from the pack to your pocket.

This principle is most ingenious, and although simple, is worthy of presentation, and done properly can be quite a puzzler to the onlookers.

Have a genuine Ace of Diamonds in your pocket to begin with, now arrange the other three Aces as in Fig. 3. The two black Aces effectively mask part of the Ace of Hearts to make it look like a Diamond.

All you do now is to turn them over and place them one at a time in the pack. There is a complete absence of false moves and the audience will think you have a duplicate Ace. They will be quite baffled when you pass the pack for inspection at the end.

TIME WILL TELL

This is an intriguing card trick that will have your friends thinking very hard. It is the sort of stunt to work when you have conditions just right, and your audience receptive to a rather lengthy routine – not the sort of trick to

Fig. 5

work in any set programme, but, put over as an impromptu item, it really will score.

Using his own pack if he wishes, a spectator is asked to shuffle it, and whilst doing so, to think of any one of the four suits. Meanwhile the performer's back is turned and he continues to instruct the spectator to remove from the pack all the cards of that particular suit. All except the King, which stays where it is.

The spectator now lays out the cards in the form of a clock face, using the Queen as twelve, the Ace as one o'clock, and so on round to the Queen again (Fig. 5). Now the spectator stares at the clock and concentrates on any time, (say for example six o'clock), which he keeps to himself.

The performer asks him to pick up the rest of the pack and further instructs him to hold it face downwards in the left hand, then to gather the cards lying on the table and place them one by one face down on top of the pack, beginning with the Ace, then the Two and so on. He will then finish with the Queen as the top card. Now concentrating on the time thought of, he is to remove that number of cards from the bottom of the pack, and place them on the top. This being done silently so that the performer has no clue whatsoever, after which the cards are neatly squared up.

The performer now turns round, finally asks the spectator to deal the whole fifty-two cards face down all over the table in a completely haphazard fashion.

Taking the spectator's hand he asks him to concentrate on both the suit and the time, and moving his hand over the cards the performer finally pushes it down onto one card.

The spectator now reveals the suit and time and when the card is turned face up it is seen to correspond exactly.

Provided you give your directions clearly to the spectator, there is very little for you to worry about until he begins to deal them face down on the table. As he does so, start counting and watch where he deals the thirteenth card, this one will represent the suit and time thought of, the rest is just showmanship.

Of course the method is simple, but it is all veiled in your presentation, using the clock face and so on. Follow the instructions given and try it out – it's a real baffler to the onlooker.

LOCO CARD

Magicians who enjoy thinking up new card tricks, try to baffle each other with their latest methods of trying to locate a card after it has been selected and lost in the pack. The beginner will soon realize that card locations in many varied forms comprise the greater part of tricks that can be performed with cards.

The Loco Card Trick is another of these locations but nevertheless quite baffling, because the card once selected is so lost amongst all the others that its identity could not possibly be known to the performer, or so it seems.

A borrowed pack is used, and the spectator is asked to remove the cards from the case and shuffle them. They are then cut into two piles, one of these being selected by the spectator, the other taken by the performer. Both these piles are shuffled again, and while the performer looks away the spectator removes any card from his packet, notes it, and drops it onto the performer's pile. The spectator is then asked to drop his cards, a few at a time, onto the performer's packet and continue to do so until all the cards are used up.

He then cuts the whole pack into as many piles as he likes and finishes by assembling the various heaps in any order he chooses. The cards neatly squared up are now handed to the performer who is immediately able to find the spectator's chosen card.

This is quite simple. All you have to do after the cards are originally cut into two piles, is to note the top card of your heap: do this whilst you shuffle. The spectator's card goes on top of this and the rest of the moves are immaterial. He drops his group of cards on top, cuts the pack into several heaps and assembles them, but when you finally receive back the cards and fan then face towards you, his selected card will be next to (below) your noted key card.

It is most unlikely that they will be separated in the cutting; in any case it is worth taking this chance.

ODDS AND EVENS

This trick is one of the few that can be repeated over and over again without any fear of detection, in fact you will even be puzzled yourself the first few times.

Using any pack, borrowed if you like, openly remove five red and five black cards. (It is best to keep to spot cards, though not absolutely essential.) Then discard the rest of the pack. Now put the two stacks of cards face to face – that is, all cards of one colour together face up and all of the other colour face down on top of them.

Using an overhand shuffle, thoroughly mix the cards, but be especially careful that none of the cards turn over while you shuffle.

Now place them behind your back and count off the top five, turning this stack of five over. Bring both stacks round to the front again. Spread them in two separate strips along the table and you will find an equal number of face-up cards in each pile. But they will all be alike in colour in each pile.

Now to repeat, reverse one of the stacks and place the two piles together again, shuffle and put them behind your back as before and repeat. You can keep on doing this ad lib. and it will always work out right.

Should the spectator wish to try, omit to reverse the stack before being placed together. Hand them to him and even if he has an inkling how to do it he will still fail miserably.

PREDICTION

The spectator is asked to shuffle the cards, then extract any twelve from the pack and to further shuffle these twelve. Whilst this is being done the performer writes a prediction on a piece of paper which is placed face down in full view on the table. The spectator now takes any four cards from his packet of twelve and lays them in a row face up on the table, the remaining eight cards being put with the rest of the pack. This is now taken up, and from it cards are dealt onto each of the face-up cards so as to bring its value to ten. For instance, if a Six you simply deal four cards on top of it. If a Three, just deal seven cards. All the Court cards, however, are valued at ten so no cards are put on these.

This having been done, the total value of the four cards is ascertained. For example, supposing the four face-up cards happen to be the Four of hearts, the Eight of Spades, the Queen of Spades and the Six of Diamonds, their total value would be twenty-eight. The card which lies at that number is now counted down to in the pack that remains. When it is turned over it is found to correspond with the original prediction.

This is one of those self-working tricks: it requires no skill and can be done with a borrowed pack – but make sure the pack is a complete one.

To 'recap' in brief: The spectator shuffles the pack and extracts any twelve cards and whilst he shuffles these you take a peep at the bottom card of the pack remaining; this is the prediction card. Write the name of this card on the paper and without showing it, put it to one side. Tell the spectator to remove any four cards discarding the rest. Drop the bulk of the pack on top of these, which brings your prediction card ninth from the bottom. The spectator lays out his four cards and deals on each one sufficient cards to make up ten. The total of the four face-up cards is obtained and this number counted down to – yes it will be the card you previously predicted. Amazing, isn't it?

CHAPTER TWO

Useful Sleights

WHEN people think of card tricks they assume automatically that sleight of hand is used. The foregoing chapter belies that fact. Reasonably good card tricks can be performed without sleight of hand, but if we were to dispense with sleights altogether most of the joy would go out of doing card tricks, for with them we can seemingly achieve miracles. Having obtained mastery over a particular sleight gives one a sense of fulfilment, and to despair just because a certain sleight seems impossible to you is wrong. Rather better to leave it for a few days and come back to it. Often you will be pleasantly surprised how easy it becomes when you try it again.

One of the annoying features of learning to do card tricks from a book is the fact that you have to turn over a page just when you have got the cards nicely set in your hand. If you possess a recorder, it is a good idea to read out what has been written – then play it back with the cards in your hand. You will then be able to listen to yourself explaining how to do it, tantamount to personal tuition in fact. Of course practice is the key word and the more practice again – but when it becomes a bore, leave it a while and come back to it fresh and with added keenness.

ABOUT THE PASS

In card magic the sleight used to cause a card to move secretly from the centre of the pack to the top or bottom, is called a pass. Naturally this term is well-known to card conjurers and the pass itself is used extensively by them. The pass forms the basis of a great many card tricks. That is why almost every book on card magic includes methods by which the pass can be executed. I must urge the beginner to endeavour, if he can, to execute the pass neatly. Once learned, it will always stand him in good stead but one cannot pretend that it is an easy sleight to master, and because such great stress has been laid on learning it, many would-be card conjurers have given up any idea of further progress, believing that without its mastery the pleasures of performing card tricks are beyond them.

Deliberately this subject has been left until later in the book, because, as you will have realized, there are many tricks, and good ones too, in which we have managed to dispense with the pass.

Nevertheless it is hoped that this book will not only teach the reader how to do various card tricks, but furnish him also with the extra knowledge needed when reading other books. He need not therefore be dismayed when he reads the words 'Have a card selected, returned to the pack bringing it to top by means of the pass,' which is exactly the way the descriptions of quite a lot of tricks begin.

It has been said earlier that the pass is used to cause a card to shift from the centre to the top or bottom of the pack, and whilst this is the actual purpose of the operation the statement is not strictly correct. What does in fact happen, is that you *transpose* the positions of the two halves of the pack, i.e. the bottom half is moved to the top and vice versa.

At first sight this would seem formidable and one finds

it difficult to visualize this movement being done invisibly or unsuspected by the onlooker. There are two ways in which this can be accomplished. The first is to endeavour to perform the sleight invisibly and silently. This calls for a degree of skill not usually envisaged by the normal person, but you must do the best you can. The second way is to execute the sleight, and although the spectators may realize that something has happened they don't know exactly what.

Quite a lot of performers delude themselves into thinking that their particular 'pass' is indetectable, silent and invisible, but a present-day audience has to be naive indeed to be gulled by it. The inference then is this: the 'pass' when executed should be camouflaged by something, and in my opinion the most logical thing is to cover it with a shuffle.

So until you attain real proficiency at the 'pass' it is suggested that you follow it immediately with a shuffle or better still combine the two. Once having got your card to the top of the pack it is comparatively easy to retain it there by means of the false shuffle.

THE PASS

Assume a card has been selected, and the pack has been divided at the point of removal; one half is held in the left hand and the other in the right. After being noted, the card is replaced on the top of the bottom half in the left hand. The pack is back upwards and held as in Fig. 6. Note that the force card is indicated by a cross.

As the top portion of the pack is replaced, insert the little finger of the left hand (Fig. 7). (The view shown is yours, not that of the audience.) The right hand immediately covers the pack grasping it with the thumb at the nearest end, the three fingers at the far end, with the tip of the forefinger just over the left side.

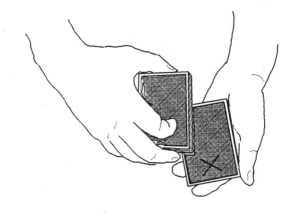

Fig. 6

This action now takes place: the right forefinger presses down on the lower portion, the upper portion is gripped firmly between the third and little finger. Right thumb presses against the near end of the lower portion, right fingers grip the far end.

The upper portion is pivoted as if opening a book, the third and little fingers being used as a lever, whilst the lower portion is pivoted, hingeing against the crook of the left hand, the right finger and thumb assisting (Fig. 8). Allow the upper portion to fall back into the left palm, whilst the lower portion is lifted sufficiently far enough up to clear, then allow to drop back on top of it (Fig. 9). The pack is squared up and the move completed.

As previously stated, the move requires some sort of cover, so go immediately into a shuffle, endeavour to blend the moves for the pass into the shuffle itself. After sufficient practice you can, if you wish, eliminate the shuffle and having executed the pass proper, immediately spread the cards into a fan. Swing both hands to the left and then from left to right as the actual spread is made.

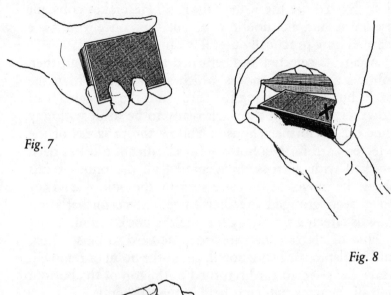

Fig. 7

Fig. 8

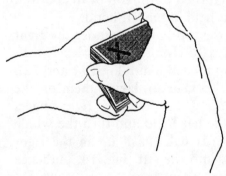

Fig. 9

THE ROLY POLY PASS

It may sometimes be thought curious that even the most adept will often resort to the simplest means to bring about a certain result; remember that the effect on the audience is the same whether you use great skill or just a clever subterfuge.

Ross Chandaue, who is a very clever card manipulator, first showed me the Roly Poly Pass. He makes constant use of it and no doubt you will too, once you have learned how practically useful it can be.

A card is selected and returned to the pack and then follows a series of moves which seem to lose it in the pack, hopelessly mixing the cards into the bargain. It is, however, on top of the pack ready to be dealt with any time the performer chooses. Follow the progress of the selected card in the photos – for clarification it has been marked with a cross. Incidentally, all the photographs show the moves as they are seen by the onlooker. They have been grouped together so that a performer's eye view is effected simply by turning the book round.

First of all, fan the cards for one card to be selected, and whilst this is being noted, cut at the point of removal. Have the selected card returned to the top of the bottom half of the pack, which is held in the left hand.

Place the left edge of the top half just under the right edge of the bottom (Fig. 10). Using this as a lever, turn the bottom half face up in the left hand (Figs. 11 and 12). Now turn the top half also face up, laying them on the now face-up bottom half (Fig. 13). With the right fingers pick up the cards from the left hand and turn the whole pack face down. The cards will finish up in the right hand, so toss them back into the left (Fig. 14: audience view), immediately fanning them from left to right. Do this in a continuous series of moves and the impression is received of losing the selected card in the pack.

But of course, as you will see from the illustrations and in actual practice, the card is safely under your control at the top of the pack.

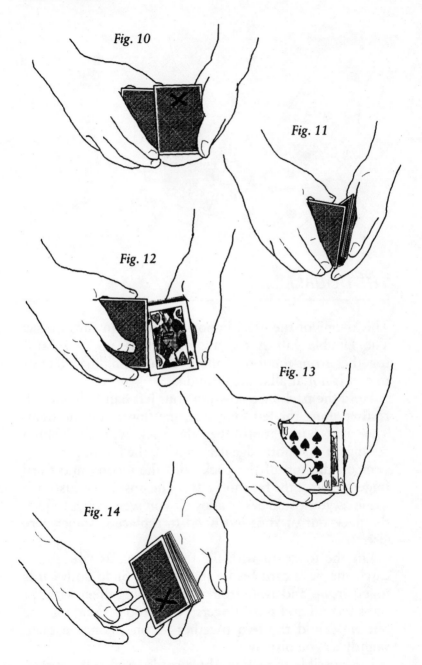

Fig. 10

Fig. 11

Fig. 12

Fig. 13

Fig. 14

Fig. 15

THE DOUBLE LIFT

This is one of the most important moves in card magic. The Double Lift is the act of picking up two cards together from the top of the pack and holding them as one. It is not at all difficult to do.

Hold the pack face down in your left hand, the thumb resting along the left long side, the fingers on the right. The right hand approaches the pack with the thumb resting on the short edge nearest you, the forefinger being bent on the top of the pack with the second and third fingers against the far short edge. The position is just such a one as you could easily adopt if you were going to pick the pack out of your left hand to replace it somewhere else.

Lift the top card with the thumb and, as you do so, catch the next card below it (Fig. 15). Slide both cards together, up and away from you, gripping them with the right second and third fingers at the top – thumb at the bottom. Hold the two together as one, concave them slightly as you display them.

It is possible to pick up three cards (triple lift) or even more in this way, although you may have to give the top few a gentle riffle with your right thumb in order to ensure the correct number being picked up. However, concentrate on the Double Lift at first.

Here is an example of a practical use for the Double Lift. Lift the top two as one, showing it as, say, the King of Spades. Replace it (them) back on top, slide off the actual top card and ask someone to blow on it, turn it over and the audience see that the King has changed to another card.

PULL THROUGH SHUFFLE

This clever false shuffle has many uses. For instance, you can keep the bottom part of the pack under control even though you subject it to the most convincing shuffle, or you can show a pack apparently to consist entirely of one card.

It is sometimes known as the Hindu Shuffle and is quite easy to do and very effective even when using a borrowed pack. Take a look at the accompanying drawings and with the pack in your hands follow the directions – you will be surprised how easy it is.

Hold the pack face up in your left hand with the thumb supporting the long side nearest you, and the four fingers resting against the far side. Your right thumb and fingers grip the right-hand end of the pack (Fig. 16). With the right thumb and fingers pull out about half the cards from the lower half of the pack (Fig. 17).

Tilt this half so the spectators get a glimpse of the bottom card (Fig. 18). Lay this half partly on those still remaining in the left hand (Fig. 19). But still retaining the grip on the end of these cards with your right fingers, withdraw a packet of cards from the lower part of this half (Fig. 20) removing them completely, then tilt so that the spectators see the bottom card. The cards which remain in the left hand are allowed to square themselves

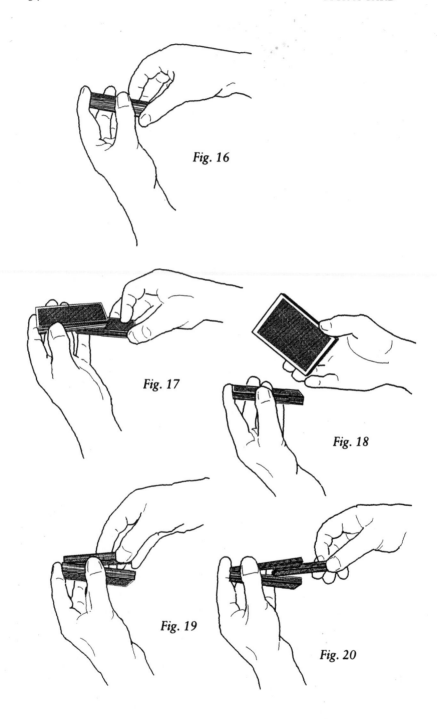

Fig. 16

Fig. 17

Fig. 18

Fig. 19

Fig. 20

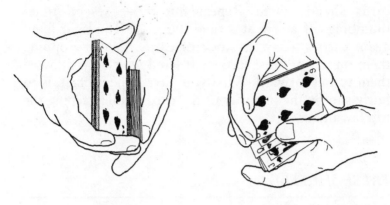

Fig. 21   Fig. 22

up. Now repeat this move, again laying the cards on top withdrawing a small packet from the centre, the left fingers assist in drawing off the cards which you leave in the left hand. Remember to show the bottom card of the right hand heap on each occasion – it will of course actually be the same card every time.

Now try the moves with the pack held face down – it will look as though you have a pack comprised of one card. You will find that you can continue the shuffle until one card remains in the right hand, the card that has been shown throughout. An interesting variation is to reverse the bottom card, and by executing the pull-through shuffle you can make the pack appear to be printed with backs on both sides.

FALSE SHUFFLE (1)

To keep the top stock of cards intact. Hold the pack in the right hand, card faces to the left just as if for normal shuffling. The left thumb slides off a group into the left hand (Fig. 21). The right comes away, then brings the cards it holds over those in the left hand sufficient for the left thumb to slide off a few more, which adds them to the cards already there. Repeat this move several times thumbing off a few at a time (Fig. 22). The right hand again carries away its stock of cards, finally dropping them on top of those in the left hand which has allowed them to fall forward. What you have done, in fact, is to fairly shuffle the majority of the cards while keeping the top few intact.

FALSE SHUFFLE (2)

To apparently shuffle the pack but to keep the cards in exactly the same order as they were at first.

This is a little difficult to achieve smoothly, and it is only by practice that you can attain a speed which will make the shuffle seem convincing. The pack can be shuffled with the backs outwards, but the illustrations show the faces in order to follow the moves more easily.

Begin by holding the cards in the right hand as in the first false shuffle. The left thumb slides off about two-thirds of the cards into the left hand as in Fig. 21. These cards are allowed to fall forward against the left fingers, while the right hand brings its stock of cards behind them and picks up a group of about half the cards held in the left hand using the base of the thumb and the third finger of the right hand (Fig. 22).

The right hand still retains a grip of its original stock (see Fig. 22 – Six of Spades). The left hand allows its stock to fall against the thumb (Fig. 23 – Jack of Clubs packet).

The original (Six of Spades) packet is now dropped on top of those in the left hand and finally allow them to fall against the left fingers so the right hand can finally deposit its stock in front of them (Fig. 24). This series of moves should be assiduously practised so that the shuffle blends into a smooth series of up-and-down movements

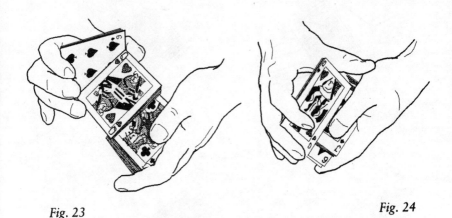

Fig. 23

Fig. 24

of the right hand. In order to assist in practise, divide the pack into three parts placing an elastic band round each – you will then see where each section should fall to maintain the order of the pack.

NOTE: Eric Mason describes another false shuffle, which will enable you to keep the top stock intact, on page 102.

Having dealt with one or two ways of keeping control of a freely selected card, we now turn to another aspect of card magic which is equally important.

In many routines it will be necessary to make a spectator 'select' a card you wish him to take even though he thinks he has made a free choice.

This is called forcing a card, there are many ways of doing this, the first one to be described is extremely simple but nevertheless quite effective.*

*See also page 83 for a description of the COUNTING FORCE and page 97 for CURLEY'S CARD FORCE.

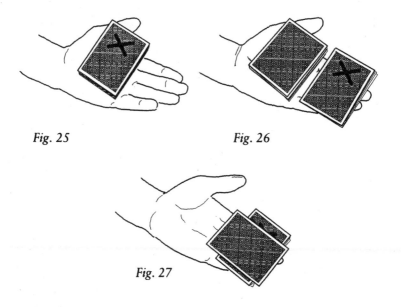

Fig. 25   Fig. 26

Fig. 27

CUT FORCE

Have the card to be forced on top of the pack, false shuffle the pack if you like but ensure that the force card stays on top.

Lay the pack on the palm of the left hand near the wrist, see Fig. 25. Note that the position of the force card is indicated by an 'x' in the sketch.

Now have a spectator cut the pack and lay this cut upper half on your hand in front of the lower half as shown in Fig. 26.

Ask him to place the lower half crosswise on the upper part as shown in Fig. 27.

Place the pack in this position on the table, this will distract the attention sufficiently to confuse the spectators as to which half is which.

Finally instruct him to lift up the top half and to look at the top card of the other half 'where he cut'. It will of course be the card you wanted him to take.

FORCING PACK

Probably the easiest way to force a card is to have a pack with all the cards the same. Obvious to you but not necessarily to the spectator. It is better to make use of such a fake pack in a platform performance rather than in a close-up presentation. After all the effect is the same and it allows you to devote more attention to the showmanship angle. However it is as well to have the bottom card of the pack different from the others in case it is glimpsed by a sharp-eyed spectator.

There will also be occasions when it will be necessary to force more than one card, for instance the THREE WAY FORCING PACK will enable you to force three different cards.

The pack is composed of three banks of like cards. Approach the first person fanning the top part of the pack. It will be easy to get him to take one from this section. Next fan the centre part of the pack for the second person to choose. Lastly spread the bottom part for the third card to be taken. From the spectators' viewpoint you have offered a pack for three cards to be taken from different parts of the deck.

Another variation of the THREE WAY PACK is to set it up as follows. We will assume that the three cards are for example, the Queen of Spades, the Ace of Clubs and the Nine of Diamonds. Lay them on top of each other in this order, on top of these another three in the same order and so on until you have a complete pack comprising of these sets of three cards repeated throughout.

Hand the pack to a spectator to cut the pack. He does this several times, finally to take the top three cards. These will be three force cards and they will all be different.

You could if you wish merely spread the cards, have him touch the fan at any point and to take three cards from this place in the spread. It seems natural to have the cards selected yet you have again successfully forced three cards.

CHAPTER THREE

Tricks Requiring Sleight-of-Hand

*H*AVE you mastered the pass yet? Can you execute a nifty double lift? They were not too difficult, were they? Well, we come now to a few tricks which will require a little slight of hand. With the exception of the Glide (Three Card Monte), the effects about to be described will involve the use of one or two sleights which have been dealt with in the last few pages.

CHAMELEON PACKS

This splendid routine w ith two packs makes use of the Pull Through Shuffle already mentioned in the previous chapter. You will require one pack with blue-backed cards and one pack with red backs.

Before you start, place a red-backed card on top of the blue-backed pack and a blue card on the red pack. Place the red cards in the blue box and the blue cards in the red box. You are now ready to work a neat little miracle. Pick up the red box and remove the cards, shuffle them with the faces to the spectators, keep the top card in position, square up the pack and replace it in the box, but rather as an afterthought, remove the top card – the red one – and lay it on top of the box. The audience will have no reason to suspect that the pack is not a red one.

Pick up the blue box – take out the cards and holding them face up execute the Pull Through Shuffle, casually show the bottom card every so often but not obviously. The cards will appear to be blue in colour. Replace them in the box, again remove one card as before (the one blue card).

So far the audience will merely assume that you have two differently coloured packs both of which you have shuffled. They will be blissfully unaware of trickery at this point but the trick is finished as far as you are concerned.

Direct someone to change over the two indicator cards, say that you will cause the packs also to change their colour and, to everyone's amazement, when they are removed the entire packs have changed to the same colour as their indicator cards, and of course both packs will withstand examination.

THE PUSH THROUGH CARD TRICK

Have a card selected, noted and returned to the pack, bring it to the top by means of the pass. (Where have we heard that phrase before?) Double-lift the top two cards and show them as one card with the face to the audience. They will see it is not their selected card. Replace the two cards on top of the pack, but immediately thumb off the actual top card, taking it in the right fingers. Put this card, still held face down, about half way in the centre of the pack. Fig. 28 shows the spectator's view of the cards which are held in the left hand – note the card protruding. This is, of course, the actual selected card – but this fact is unsuspected by the audience.

Now take any card from somewhere near the top of the pack, show it, then insert it likewise but below the first protruding card. Place it so that only one or two cards come between them. Turn the pack face up drawing attention to the bottom card which is then removed. Turn the pack face down and insert this card above the two cards already there. Again allow only a few cards to come between. Fig. 29 will make this quite clear.

As far as the audience is concerned you have merely taken three different cards, none of which is the selected card, and these three remain protruding from the pack. The centre card is of course the selected card.

Now ask someone to pinch the ends of the protruding cards together and at the same time to push them into the pack (Fig. 30). This will have the effect of pushing out a block of cards to the rear, so with the right forefinger you push this block back in again. This action will in turn cause one card to project at the front (Fig. 31). Ask a spectator to remove it and to his surprise it will be the actual, originally selected card.

If you follow the instructions with the cards in your hands you will be amused at the uncanny way in which the card appears at the end. The effect can be heightened by covering the cards with a silk handkerchief during the 'pushing' operations, the whole thing being done under cover which makes the eventual climax even greater.

THREE CARD MONTE

Three cards are shown and examined, one of them a Queen. They are *slowly* counted face up and then slowly turned face down, yet the spectator is never able to pick out the Queen. This plot is basic to all other Three Card Trick routines, but it differs in the respect that the cards are shown face up until the last second, and with the absence of any quick moves they are turned face down, yet the spectators are baffled every time.

Two spot cards and a Queen are all that are required, but the effect can be enhanced by the addition of one or two subtle devices to be explained later.

Although sleight of hand is employed to bring about the effect, the only two sleights needed have been put to

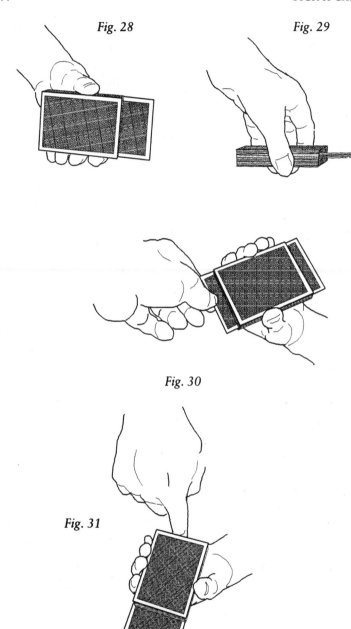

Fig. 28

Fig. 29

Fig. 30

Fig. 31

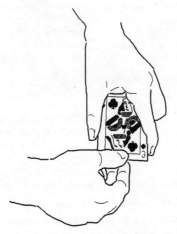

Fig. 32

the most ideal use and are extremely simple to perform. The sleights are the Double Lift and the Glide, and they will be explained as we go along.

Begin by displaying the three cards, drawing attention to the Queen.

(1) Show them back and front – let someone examine them if desired. The spectators see that you only have three cards and that they are quite ordinary.

(2) Hold them in the left hand face up with the Queen on top. The palm should be towards the floor. The forefinger rests along the left long side of the cards whilst the thumb supports the cards at about the centre of the right long side (Fig. 32). The second finger lightly touches the back of the bottom card, just below the centre.

(3) *The Glide*: slide the bottom card back to the left with the tip of the second finger (moisten if necessary). The forefinger and thumb allows this card to slide evenly – let it slide back about half an inch, as in Fig. 33 which shows a worm's-eye view of this move, and note the position of the second finger.

(4) Now let the right hand approach, and with the palm uppermost, grip the top two cards between the forefinger and thumb – the thumb on top, as in Fig. 33.

Left fingers
executing the glide

Fig. 33

You have now executed the Glide and this will allow you to *double lift* the top two cards as one quite effortlessly.

(5) With the right hand slide the top two cards away to the right revealing the bottom card. At this stage the spectators will think that you have merely lifted away the top card (Queen). The Glide and Double Lift should be executed simultaneously.

(6) Position is now: The left hand holds one card face up (spectators think there are two cards there). Right hand holds two cards face up (spectators think there is only one card there). Left palm faces downwards, right palm faces upwards.

Now turn over both hands so that the cards appear face downwards.

Fig. 34 shows the act of turning the hands over. The left hand card is about to be turned downwards and the cards in the right hand are laid on top of it.

(7) Repeat these moves several times, always executing the Glide and Double Lift. Finish up with the Queen apparently in the centre (actually it will be on top).

(8) Fan the three cards face down and invite someone to pick out the Queen. They will pick out the wrong card each time. Do the trick a few times, then finally offer to help them with their selection.

Take a paper clip from your pocket. Show the cards, again drawing attention to the Queen when it comes into view. Slowly place it on top face down as before and immediately push it to the right with your left thumb and

Fig. 34

attach the paper clip to it. Of course it will not actually be the Queen, but if done very slowly and deliberately the spectators will really think the clip is on the Queen.

Now move the three cards around once more, inviting someone to pick up the Queen and in spite of the clip locator they will fail once again.

The final subtlety with the Three Card Monte makes a very clever use of the one-way pattern sometimes found as the back design on some types of cards. Cards with a definite picture on the back makes the obvious one-way back cards, so that if you started with a pack with the design all one way and reversed one of them you would easily be able to pick it out.

Begin by having the three cards in a fan. The Queen is in the centre – turn over the fan to show this, then slowly reverse the Queen so that its design faces the other way. Turn them face upwards with the Queen in the centre. Do the Double Lift and Glide four times showing the cards as before; this will leave the Queen apparently in the centre of the face-down fan. The spectators are more certain, because this card has its back design one-way pattern reversed. However, when the card is picked out once more it is seen to be anything but the Queen.

CARD SPREAD

Can you 'spread' a pack of cards? Well, most people can – if you have a new pack and it can be done by merely

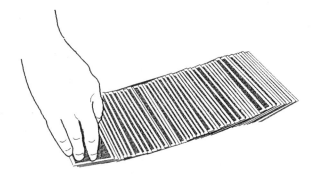

Fig. 35

sliding them – but take a look at Fig. 35 and you will see how easy it is when done the professional way.

Notice how the cards are held in the right hand, as they are spread from left to right, the thumb at the near end, forefinger resting on top of the pack, the second and third fingers hold the top end.

Pinch the ends of the cards upwards – applying also a slight pressure on the top of the pack with the forefinger. This will cause the cards to become concave.

Spread the cards and as you do so allow them to drop singly. Practise spreading the cards – it is quite a good flourish and looks far more clever than it really is.

TURNOVER REVERSE

Here is an effective trick with uses the 'spread' to bring about the effect.

Fan a pack of cards for one to be selected, then have it returned to the pack. Use the Roly Poly Pass (see page 29) to bring it to the top. Now Double Lift the two cards as one, show them to the audience. Say 'Is this your card?'

After receiving a negative reply, replace them back on the top of the pack but immediately thumb off the actual top card and keeping it still face down, place it aside on

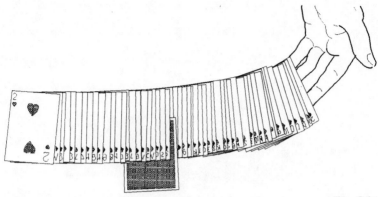

Fig. 36

the table. Taking the pack in the right hand turn it over so that it is face up, then ribbon-spread them on the table. Insert the selected card face down into the face-up spread just about the centre – just tuck the card a little way into the spread (Fig. 36).

The position as the spectator will see it is this – the pack is spread face up along the table, but there is one card at about the centre of the spread face down: they know this is not their card. You ask for their card to be named and at the same time you flick over the bottom card of the spread, thus causing all the cards to reverse (Figs. 37, 38, 39). All the cards are now face down except one and this is the card originally selected staring them in the face.

ONE OVER THE EIGHT

Some time ago Peter Kane introduced to the magical fraternity an ingenious card routine and called it the Wild Card. Since then, conjurers the world over have been performing different versions of Kane's trick.

The following is a further adaptation, part of the handling of which is also credited to my friend Eddie Tatelbaum of Holland, the use of the short card principle

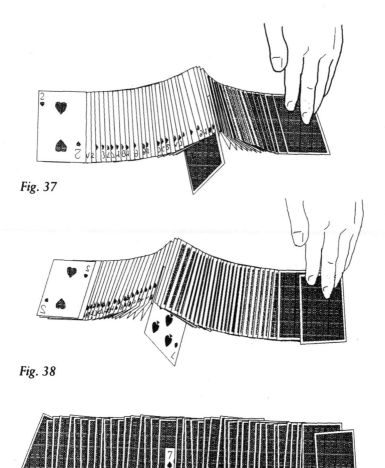

Fig. 37

Fig. 38

Fig. 39

I discovered quite by accident, and this is the part that
makes the working that much simpler.

This trick ranks among the best of card tricks because
it is extremely visual, and is really most baffling to the
audience.

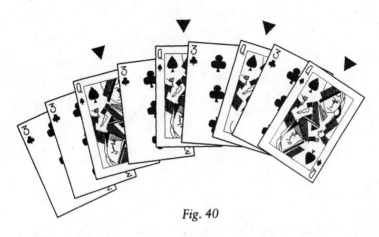

Fig. 40

The effect is quite straightforward, and what the audience sees is eight cards all alike, these are shown back and front, but an extra card of a different value is used to transform all the eight cards to cards of the same value as itself.

You will therefore require nine cards, five of these are all alike and they are quite ordinary except that they have been slightly shortened. The other four cards are normal length but they are double-faced, one side matches the five short cards; the other side has a completely different denomination.

The illustration (Fig. 40) shows the five shortened cards as Threes of Clubs whilst the double-faced cards are Queens of Spades on one side and of course Threes of Clubs on the reverse. They are indicated in the sketch by four white arrows.

The faked cards are readily available in magic shops but at the end of this chapter a method of preparing double-faced cards is described.

The cards are set up for the trick as follows: lay them face up on the table from left to right in the following order (see also Fig. 40). Two ordinary Threes of Clubs, then on top of these place a double-facer with the opposite value showing (Q.S.). Next an ordinary card

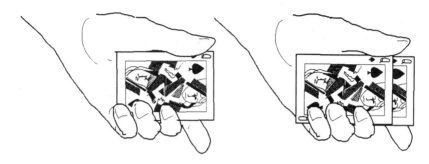

Fig. 41   *Fig. 42*

(3 C.) followed by a double-face (Q.S.), then a Three of
Clubs, and on this a double-face (Q.S.). Now the last
Three of Clubs, and finally the last double-faced Queen
of Spades. As mentioned before the illustration shows
little black pointers which indicate the double-faced
cards. Slide them together in a stack and you are ready to
work the effect.

Begin by holding the stack of cards face up in the left
hand as shown in Fig. 41.

Draw attention to the bottom card and name it (Q.S.).
Now turn the left hand face down and glide back the
bottom card to your left with the tip of the left second
finger.

The right finger and thumb approaches and takes the
next card up (3. C.) and lays it face down on the table.
The spectators, of course, think that this is the (Q.S.).

Keeping the original bottom card still held back, turn
over the left hand face up to show the bottom card and
the next one up in a stepped fashion, see Fig. 42. The
audience see them as both Queens of Spades. Now openly
take the actual bottom card and lay it face up on the table
below the face-down card already there.

Turn the left hand face down once more and repeat the
same move, that is to glide the bottom card back, and

Fig. 43

pick off the next one up, laying it face down alongside the other one on the table.

Turn the hand face up showing the cards stepped as before, only Queens of Spades being seen.

Again openly take the actual bottom card and place it face up alongside the other face-up card on the table.

Do the same with the third and fourth pairs so that the eight cards are seen on the table as shown in Fig. 43. (The double-faced cards are again indicated by the little black pointers in the sketch.)

One row of four cards is face up, the other face down. The spectators think that they are all Queens of Spades, the one still left in the hand is seen to be the 'odd' card, the Three of Clubs.

Using this (3 C.) as a lever, turn over one of the face-down cards, and the audience will now see that it has changed to a Three of Clubs. Go along the line of face-down cards transforming them into all Threes of Clubs. Leave them face up in a row.

The situation at this point is as in Fig. 44. There is a row of four face-up Threes of Clubs and beneath them a

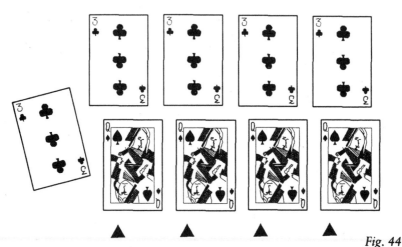

Fig. 44

row of face-up Queens of Spades. The odd card is the Three of Clubs.

Now pick up the first (Q.S.) and drop it face up on top of the first (3 C.) then lay the odd (3 C.) on top of these.

Pick up all three together holding them face up in the left hand. Openly turn over the top card face down, then square them up. Now turn the top two over as one. This is easily accomplished because of the use of the long and short cards.

Replace these two (double-lifted) cards face up on the face-up card still in the left hand, and immediately slide the top one away onto the table – it is seen to be a Three of Clubs.

Turn over the next card showing it on both sides – it is also a Three of Clubs. Finally the card remaining in the left hand is openly and deliberately turned over showing both sides and of course this is also seen as a Three of Clubs.

Repeat the same moves along the line of the remaining three Queens of Spades transforming them all into Threes of Clubs.

Finally gather all the cards together once more, fanning

them to show that they are all alike. Close the fan and drop them into your pocket.

HOW TO MAKE DOUBLE-FACED CARDS

There are two convenient ways to make them yourself. The first to be described is the easiest but it has the slight disadvantage of taking the natural polish off the cards. However they can be restored by spraying a thin film of wax silicone polish over them, then polish with a soft cloth.

Incidentally this is a good dodge to use when you wish any cards to be more slippery. These are known as smooth cards.

The cards which are to be split are laid on the surface of a bowl of clean water and left for several hours or overnight. After this period you will be surprised to see that the cards have separated themselves into two halves.

Remove them from the water and lay them on a clean towel allowing them to dry naturally. Do not use heat or they will curl and crinkle. When dry the card halves can be glued together as desired.

The other method takes a little patience but is very effective and after one or two attempts you will find that you will become quite adept at it.

Take the card to be split and bruise one corner by tapping it on the table. You will find that the card can be separated at this point, a needle or the point of a sharp knife assisting. Carefully peel away one layer. Most playing cards are comprised of three layers, the face and the back, and sandwiched between them is a stiffer layer usually of a different colour.

Decide which side you wish to preserve and lay this face down on the table then slowly roll away the two upper layers together.

Having got your thin layers of various cards you can

now re-glue them again according to the combinations required.

Of course, in this manner you are able to make other fake cards such as Double-Backed and those with different coloured sides and so on.

CHAPTER FOUR

Tricks using Apparatus

*I*T is now comparatively easy for the conjurer to send away for any of the countless pieces of apparatus available for sale in the magic shops. For instance, one can buy the necessary equipment to cause a card to appear in a balloon, or innumerable trick packs of cards which will enable the performer to constantly ring the changes in his repertoire. Special fakes are available to make cards vanish and appear at the fingertips – or to mysteriously diminish them at will. There are colour-changing packs – packs all alike – packs with holes in them – packs of peculiar shapes and so on, ad infinitum. They all serve the purpose of enabling the conjurer to present new and different tricks in his endeavour to entertain people. This next chapter deals with three card tricks requiring apparatus, but not to worry, because the items required can easily be procured or made.

THE CARD IN THE WALLET

Over the years conjurers have attempted to find new ways to make selected cards leave the pack and be found in the most unlikely places, inside cigarettes, oranges, walnuts, picture frames, on ceilings, at the end of swords and so on. Their ingenuity is limitless. A classic among these transpositions, as they are called, is the Card in the Wallet. There are many ways to perform this effect, but I am sure you will use the following method.

This is the effect: A spectator selects a card from which a corner is torn and he keeps this for later identification. The magician removes his wallet and lays it in full view on the table. Now the selected card is openly torn into little pieces and these are dropped into an envelope, but suddenly this is torn open – the pieces have vanished! The magician blithely opens his wallet and extracts the self-same card – fully restored minus the corner which is found to match exactly with the piece which was in possession of the spectator the whole time.

You will require a duplicate card in your pack, and a fake envelope made as described later. Also a specially prepared wallet as follows. An ordinary leather type pocket wallet will do: using a razor blade, cut a slit lengthwise in one side. This slit should be about 5 in. long and run parallel to one of the long edges of the wallet about ½in. inwards.

If a card is held under the wallet which is slit side to the floor you should be able to open it and reach into the inner compartment and extract the card. Your fingers go right through the slit pulling the card through. The illusion is perfect, and some wallets have a zip fastener in the centre making it most effective to open the wallet unzipping and then extracting the card.

One final point before we pass on to the working; you will need to stick a small blob of wax at the centre on the slit side of the wallet – the purpose of this will become apparent later.

Begin by false shuffling the pack, the top two cards are the two duplicate cards. One of these is forced (see page 37), noted and replaced on top of the pack, so the two like cards are together again. At this point refer to the stack of envelopes, then go back to the cards, pick up the top two as one (Double Lift). Tear off the corner of both cards together (Fig. 45), hand the 'corner' to the spectator – but as you do so, slide one of them down into your

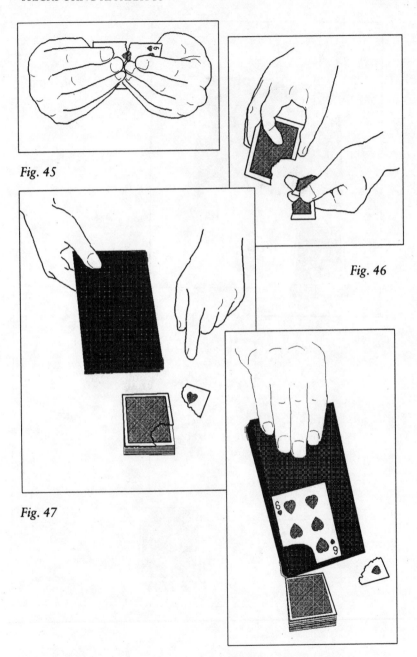

Fig. 45

Fig. 46

Fig. 47

Fig. 48

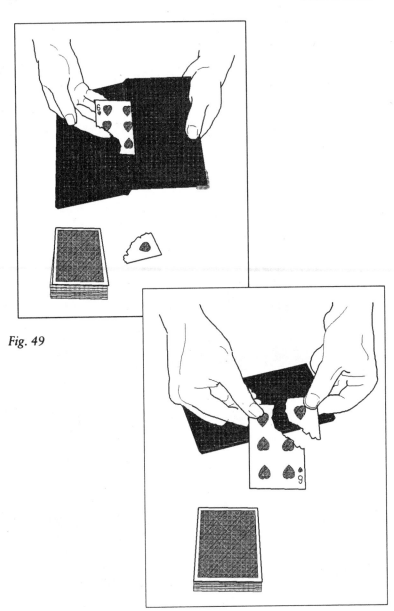

Fig. 49

Fig. 50

hand. Fig. 46 shows *your* view of this action. Place the two cards back on top of the pack – remember that the spectators think there is only one card there. Reach into your pocket, leave the palmed duplicate corner behind and take out your wallet. Casually place it on top of the pack, slit side downwards, the spot of wax coming into contact with the top card.

Making it seem an after-thought, lift the wallet off again and gesture with it to the top card saying, 'It will make the trick harder if you tear the card up completely.' (Fig. 47.) Lay the wallet down, but of course it has carried away with it the top card (Fig. 48 – your view). However, the second card will still be there and the spectators have no reason to suspect foul play at this point. This card is torn up into little pieces, and these are dropped into the top envelope (see 'Envelope Switch') and is apparently taken from its packet, sealed, and placed on the table.

The trick is almost done – the envelope is torn open – the pieces have vanished. Pick up the wallet, reach into it through the slit, remove the card (Fig. 49). Hand it to the spectator to verify that his small piece really fits (Fig. 50). While this is being done, casually pocket the wallet, pick up the envelopes and you are at liberty to bask in the reflected glory of super-magical mystery.

ENVELOPE SWITCH

This is a useful device to enable you to exchange cards, photos, etc. in a subtle fashion.

The spectators see you genuinely place a card into an envelope and they sign the flap to identify it. Later, however, the envelope which still bears the initial is found to be empty.

Buy some seed or wage envelopes, gently open out one, and refold and restick it so it is just a trifle narrower; the

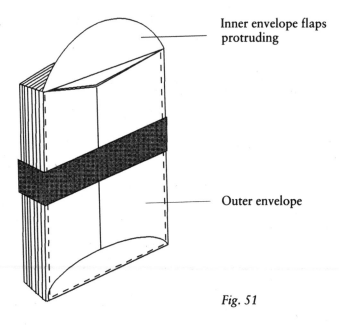

Inner envelope flaps
protruding

Outer envelope

Fig. 51

idea being that it should slide easily in and out of another
envelope. Cut the flap off the other envelope and place
the smaller one inside it (Fig. 51). The fake pair of
envelopes is put on top of the stack and a band placed
round them.

Suppose you wish to vanish the torn pieces of a card.
Openly place them in the envelope – actually they go into
the outside one but have the flap initialled on both sides
at this stage – turn over the stack and pull out the inner
envelope, seal it and put it in a prominent place. Eventually this envelope can be inspected – the initials verified.
But of course it will be found empty.

You will see that this excellent switch can be utilized in
a variety of effects. For instance, you can make a message
appear mysteriously on a blank piece of paper – change a
blank card into a genuine one – or put a treasury note in
the envelope, burn it and reproduce the note elsewhere.

THE CARD PLAQUES

This is quite a stunning effect because a selected playing card makes a surprise appearance between two squares of cardboard which have previously been shown on all sides.

The plaques are securely fastened together with elastic bands and held by a spectator, but even under these conditions the chosen card inexplicably arrives between them.

First of all, let us deal with the plaques, which are made from stiff cardboard. Cut six pieces 5 in. square as in Fig. 52. Stick three of the pieces together to form a stiff board (Fig. 53). From one of the remaining three pieces cut out a portion just a trifle longer and a little wider than a playing card (Fig. 54). Now glue all three pieces together with the cut-out portion in the centre (Fig. 55).

You will also require a duplicate card. This is placed in the slot of the fake plaque. The only other requirements are some elastic bands and an ordinary pack with a duplicate of your force card on top.

Now to present the trick. Have the two plaques resting against a tumbler, the fake plaque with the slot side upwards (Fig. 56). Pick up each plaque, then slowly and deliberately show every side, keeping your fingers over the slot to prevent the card from falling out (Fig. 57). Place the two plaques together, fake one underneath with the slot to the right (Fig. 58). Hold them almost vertically, slide the top plaque to the right (Fig. 59). The card will slide out of the slot, but keep it pressed against the back of the upper plaque with the right fingers. Show the left-hand (faked) plaque both sides, then place it underneath the right-hand plaque with the card secretly in between. Now have someone snap elastic bands securing the two plaques together, giving them to him to hold.

The rest of the effect involves false shuffling the cards,

forcing the duplicate card and making it vanish. Finally, having the plaques separated so that the card is found between them.

Of course you could construct the plaques in thin plywood or plastic – be sure the slot is smooth on the inside to enable the card to slide out easily.

TWO WAYS TO VANISH A CARD

Short Card Method

One of the simplest ways to make a card disappear is to use a short card. This is easily made by neatly trimming a normal-sized card at the top. After having the card noted, it is returned to the pack which is shuffled, and then slowly riffled, faces to the audience. The card being shortened will slip by without being seen.

Waxed Card Method

Place a small piece of wax on the back of the Joker, and after your card is selected and noted, it is returned to the pack, but see that it goes on top of the Joker. Square up the pack and slowly deal the cards face up and singly onto the table. The two cards will stick together and are dealt as one. Then you are able to go right through the pack without revealing the card, which seems to have vanished.

Another method to make a card vanish from the pack is described under the title of 'The Card Vanishing Case', on page 99.

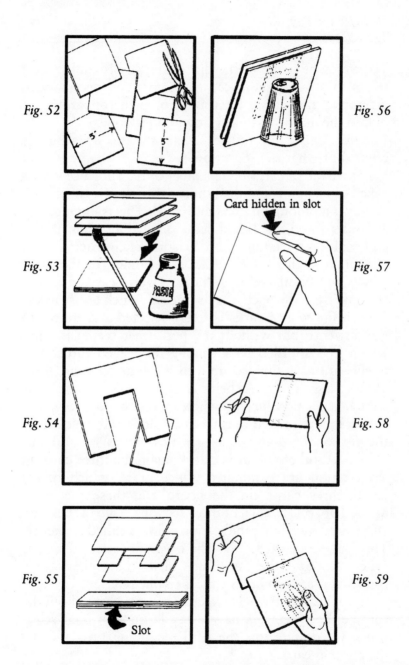

Fig. 52

Fig. 53

Fig. 54

Fig. 55

Fig. 56

Fig. 57

Fig. 58

Fig. 59

Card hidden in slot

Slot

'YOUR CARD, SIR'

To overcome some of the difficulties in presenting card tricks to a large audience, it is sometimes necessary to glamorize the effect by using colourful apparatus to obtain the utmost visibility and interest appeal.

'Your Card, Sir' utilizes what is basically a simple effect, but what the spectators see is this: The performer hands a pack of cards to a member of the audience who is asked to examine and then thoroughly shuffle them.

Now an oblong board is displayed. This is mounted on a slender stand, the board being divided into four differently coloured sections. Cord elastic stretches across each segment and this serves to act as a holder for the cards which will be placed there later. Twelve cards are now counted from the pack, the balance of which is discarded. One of the twelve cards is freely selected and shown to the audience but without the performer seeing it, after which it is shuffled back among the eleven cards. The twelve are now divided up into the four sections, three cards to a section, these being clipped backs out under the stretched elastic which now holds them in place (Fig. 60).

Someone is invited to call out a colour and the cards in the section of that colour are now removed and discarded. Another colour is called, again the three cards in that section are eliminated. Once more, which finally leaves three cards on the board and these are again divided up, one to each of three sections. Two of these are eliminated by having the section colours called as before. This leaves one card only. The originally selected card is called out and the performer turns the solitary card round. It is seen to be exactly the same one.

This trick is extremely effective because throughout the routine the spectators have every latitude in their selections, yet despite this the card remaining proves to be their actual card.

The board is easily constructed from plywood or thick

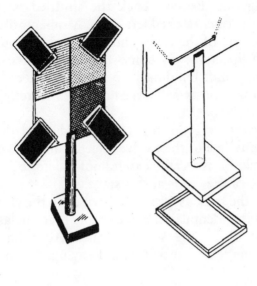

Fig. 60 · *Fig. 61*

cardboard, and measures about 10 x 7 in. It is mounted on a piece of dowelling about 6 in. high which is in turn attached to the base.

The base is faked by having a recess beneath it secretly to contain twelve cards. The simplest way to make this, is to construct a frame just large enough to fit round a playing card, using square beading about 3/16 in. high. Then glue a piece of 5-ply on top of the frame, to the top of which is fixed the dowel. Finally secure the board to the top of the dowel and paint it in bright distinctive colours. Fig. 60 shows it clearly. Notice how a length of elastic is threaded so as to form a clip at each corner of the board. (Fig. 61 shows the reverse side of the board.) Your final requirements are a pack of cards and twelve extra cards all alike. These twelve forcing cards are placed in the base ready to work the trick.

When you come to present the effect, begin by passing the cards for shuffling. Meanwhile, pick up the stand in the right hand holding the base so as to prevent the cards

from falling out. Receive back the shuffled pack face
down on your outstretched left palm. Momentarily place
the stand on top of the cards and gesture with your right
hand for a spectator to come forward to assist you.
Remove the stand, handing it to your volunteer helper;
the twelve force cards will have now been secretly added
to the top of the pack.

Openly count off the top twelve – discard the rest.
Now have any one of the twelve selected and noted, then
shuffled back. Be especially careful not to let the audience
see the faces of the cards at this stage.

Continue the trick as already described in the effect. All
the cards being identical, it is inevitable that the last card
remaining will be the selected card. After having it
named, dramatically turn it round saying, 'Your Card,
Sir!'.

CHAPTER FIVE

Miscellaneous Tricks

*A*S we have progressed through this book it will have been noted that the easiest (though not necessarily least effective) items were dealt with first. We have made the transition from easy tricks with a borrowed pack, then the sleights and so on, to this section which can be classed under the heading of 'Miscellaneous'.

Little has been said about showmanship, but none the less it is all-important, especially with regard to card tricks. If they are presented in a dull lifeless fashion, the audience, those on the receiving end, can hardly be blamed for becoming bored. Try to avoid this at all costs – keep your performance alive – vary the effects, avoid complicated long-drawn-out routines and remember it is always best to leave your audience wanting more. Perhaps the varied items which follow will help you to attain this end.

MIRACULOUS TRANSPOSITION

Sooner or later you will be recognized as an expert with a pack of cards and wherever you go people will expect you to perform marvellous tricks with them. This is just the sort of card trick which will enhance your reputation. Miraculous Transposition seems a high sounding title for a mere card trick, but the effect is truly astounding.

Imagine yourself entering a room where several of your

friends are gathered and eventually you are asked to show them your latest miracle.

Removing two packs from your pocket, you hand one to Tom and the other to Dick requesting them to take out the cards and cut them any number of times. Having done this, you further instruct them each to count off twenty-six cards onto the table in front of them – the remainder of the pack to be placed in their pockets for safe keeping. Tell Tom to hand his cards to Harry, and Dick likewise gives his cards to Bill. Harry and Bill now look through their respective packs and mentally note any card. They tell no one this thought-of card but are to firmly fix it in their mind. Harry and Bill shuffle their packs, which you take saying that you are now going to cause their mentally selected cards to vanish from the packs to appear among those cards held by Tom and Dick.

You ask Harry and Bill to put the packs back in their pockets keeping a firm hand on them. Tom and Dick meanwhile are also holding their packs in a similar fashion.

Harry names his card and Tom runs through his cards and sure enough finds it there. Bill now names his card and Dick also finds that card amongst his. Harry and Bill both look for their cards in their packs, but of course they have vanished.

If this trick is done properly people will talk about it for weeks, and on the face of it the effect does seem impossible because the cards never at any time leave the possession of Tom or Dick.

Everyone will want to examine the packs afterwards and this they can do with no one being any the wiser.

The secret is blatantly simple and only a slight preparation is needed. You require the two packs of cards but each of them is made up of two similar lots of cards, set up in the same order.

That is to say you take twenty-six different cards from one pack and the same twenty-six from the other and in exactly the same order. Put the two halves on top of each other, assembling the second pack in exactly the same way.

When Tom and Dick cut their packs at the commencement the rotation order of the cards will not be disturbed. They each deal off twenty-six cards and pass them to Harry and Bill respectively. Each looks through his pack and chooses his card.

At this point you take the packs from them and go over what has taken place in order to misdirect their attention. Place one pack crosswise on the other, holding them both in one hand for a few seconds – gesture with the other, drawing the spectators' attention to the fact that the original halves have not left the possession of Tom and Dick.

This is the only fake move – when you return the cards to Harry and Bill, see that they get the opposite halves.

The trick is now done. When they sort through the packets, the cards they thought of will have vanished miraculously, finding their way into the other halves of the pack.

PHOTOGRAPHIC THOUGHT

This card trick is quite definitely out of the ordinary. People will remember it, and more especially you, for a long time after.

A card is selected and the selector is asked to remember its value and to show it to the other members of the audience. It is now returned to the pack which is shuffled. Placing the pack behind your back, you remove one card showing it to the audience and asking if it was the card selected. Slightly crestfallen when you get a negative answer, you request the spectator to hold out his hand, and placing the card on it ask him to concentrate on his original card selected. Tell him to imagine it is printed on your forehead. When he thinks he sees it there (in his imagination, of course) he turns over the card he has in his hand. This is seen to have changed to a photograph of yourself but on your forehead in the photo is a miniature reproduction of the actual card selected.

You will need to prepare a special photo card, but the effect is well worth the time taken. Obtain a good photo of yourself and stick it to the face side of the Joker, then trim it down to the size of the card. Having done this, trim a further piece from the top making it slightly shorter than the rest. With indian ink neatly draw a miniature card on the forehead.

Any card will do but make it an easy one to draw. Put the photo card somewhere in the centre of the pack, with the card the same as the one on the forehead immediately above it. You are now all ready and set to perform.

If you prefer you can give the pack a casual shuffle, but see that the two cards are not separated and that they remain near the centre.

Tell your spectator that you are going to riffle the cards and he is to say 'Stop' at any time. Actually what happens is that you quickly riffle until you come to the photo; this will be thicker and shorter than the rest, and the cards will cause a distinct break at that point. Try to coincide your break with when he says 'Stop'. This is not as difficult as it sounds (see Fig. 62). The arrow on the back of the card in this picture indicates where the photo-card is.

The position will now be that the bottom card of those held in the right hand will be the force card (say Four of Clubs as in Fig. 63) and ask the spectator to remember it. Now replace the cards and shuffle, then put them behind your back. Immediately locate the photo by means of the riffle, and bring it to the top of the pack. Lift off the top two cards and hold them as one, using the Double Lift. Bring them round to the front and hold them slightly bowed (as in Fig. 64). The spectators will never guess that

Fig. 62

you have two cards there. Say 'Is this your card?' and of course he will tell you that it is not.

You casually drop these onto the remainder of the pack which should be held in your left hand. Look disappointed and thumb it off again (actually it will only be the photo this time), and laying it face down on his upturned palm say, 'Never mind, just concentrate on your card – not this one but the card you originally selected. Imagine it is printed on my forehead.' Have him concentrate really hard until he says he can see it there, then get him to turn over the card and he will be most surprised to see that it has changed to a photo. When he looks closer he will see a miniature reproduction of the selected card on your forehead in it.

This can be used as a grand publicity item and a good idea is to have a quantity of photos specially done so that you can leave one with the spectator every time you do the trick.

THE THREE CARD TRICK

There are certain card tricks which seem to have a greater appeal to the general public than others, and the Three

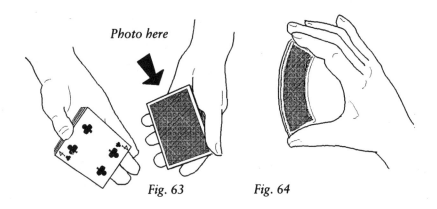

Photo here

Fig. 63   *Fig. 64*

Card Trick is one.* Perhaps its popularity is due to the extremely simple plot. Basically, the effect is that three cards, one of which is a Queen, are moved around face down and the audience try to guess where the Queen is.

If it were a mere game of chance they would have one chance in three of winning, but the conjurer cunningly brings his skill into play and the spectator seldom wins.

Sometimes known as the Three Card Monte, it is also popular with the gambling fraternity for obvious reasons, but their method involves intricate sleight of hand. However, we will concern ourselves with two ingenious methods which make use of fake cards, and cards you can easily construct yourself.

You will need three ordinary cards and a Queen. Begin by carefully cutting the Queen card lengthwise down the centre, then glue it on the face of one of the ordinary cards as shown in Fig. 65. Apply the glue at the bottom only, leaving the top portion of the 'half Queen' free.

Now make this fake card a 'short' card by trimming about 1/16 in. from the top. Round the corners nicely and your fake is ready.

* See also THREE CARD MONTE, page 43 and THE VANISHING LADY, page 77.

Trim fake card short

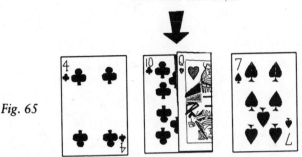

Fig. 65

Hold the three cards face down in the left hand, the fake card at the top. The fake half-Queen should lie to the left, so that when you count the cards from hand to hand it can be felt with the finger, thus telling you it is in the correct position to begin with.

Count them, showing the back of each card individually but keeping them in the same order. Now turn the cards face up, again holding them loosely on the fingers of the left hand, the fake card at the bottom with the half Queen lying to the right.

The right hand fingers at the top, thumb at the bottom, bend the ends of the cards down so that they become slightly convex.

The next move is very deceptive. Simply slide the cards apart; the left hand moves a little to the left whilst the right hand moves slightly to the right. This action will cause the two top cards to keep together as one, whilst the bottom fake card shows apparently as two. The Queen appears to be in the centre of the fan of three.

Hold them with a slight pressure of the left thumb as in Fig. 66. This illustration shows the view as the audience see it. The right thumb and forefinger now 'tweaks' the left corner of each card drawing attention to them, and you name each card as you do so. Be sure to hold them with the top edges down and away from you in order to prevent the spectators catching a glimpse of the underside of the fan.

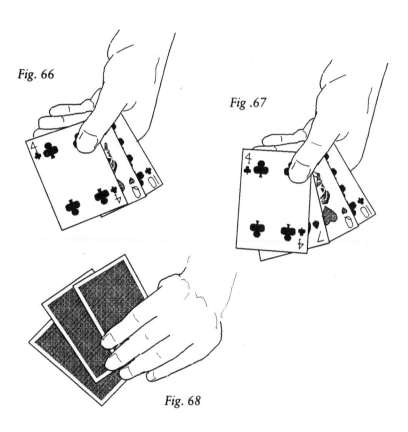

Fig. 66

Fig .67

Fig. 68

The audience takes note that the Queen is the centre card and then you turn the fan face down, simultaneously with this, however, the left thumb slides the top card to the right. Practise this move until it is imperceptible. The spectators will now see three cards face down, the centre one of which is thought to be the Queen but when it is picked out it proves to be one of the ordinary cards. Fig. 67 presents a worm's-eye view of the cards: there seem to be four but of course the audience are unable to see this and their view is of the back of the cards as in Fig. 68.

To repeat the trick, have the selected card returned to the fan of three which are held face down, counting them again as before. Locate the fake card again by feel, make

sure that it lies in the correct position and you are ready
to show the trick again.

Practise the moves until you know this routine back-
wards, and you will have one of the best of all non-slight
versions of this age-old effect. Do not despise it because
of its simplicity. It has been worked and sold in the street
market for many years, and when shown by an expert
can pass for slight of hand of the highest order. It was a
miracle in the hands of the late Charles Edwards, the
street performer.

THE VANISHING LADY

Three cards are shown back and front, the centre one is a
Queen. They are now closed together and slowly turned
face down and each card is placed separately on the table.
There can be no doubt in the spectator's mind where the
Queen is, but when it is turned over it has vanished and a
blank card is seen in its place. The other two cards are
turned over but there is still no trace of the Queen.
However, reaching into his pocket, the performer
extracts it and now all the cards are passed for thorough
inspection.

Fake cards are made use of in this version of Find The
Lady. You will require a blank face card – that is a card
printed with a back design in the ordinary way, but
where the pips or face should be it is perfectly blank.
Blank face packs are now freely available in the magic
shops, but one can easily be made by pasting a piece of
opaque white paper onto the face of an ordinary card.
Another little fake must be prepared however, and a
glance at Fig. 69 will make this quite clear. It consists of
the top portion cut from the Queen card and hinged by
means of Sellotape to the top of another card. A duplicate
of this Queen should be in your pocket and your final
requirements are just two ordinary cards.

Fig. 69

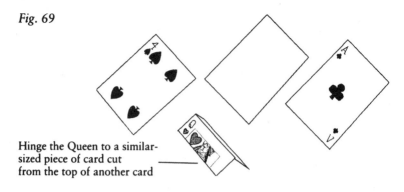

Hinge the Queen to a similar-
sized piece of card cut
from the top of another card

First of all, place the Queen fake or gimmick over the top of the blank card, the Queen at the front the back part of the fake over the back. Now place one ordinary card above and below the faked blank card; then arrange them 'stepped' fashion holding them in the left hand as in Fig. 70. In this position you are able to freely show the three cards back and front. Draw attention to the Queen in the centre – then slowly close the three cards together. Turn them face down and place them into the closed left hand. Withdraw the top card and place it face down on the table (Fig. 71). The next card will be the blank; withdraw this but leave the fake Queen part behind. Place it blank side down on the table and without showing it. The spectators will think this is the Queen. Finally, withdraw the last card, placing it likewise alongside the other on the table. This effectively leaves the fake in quite a convenient palming position. Fig. 72 gives a worm's-eye view of the fake thus palmed.

Casually drop your hand to the side and pointing with the right hand ask the spectator to pick out the Queen. When it is turned up, a blank; have the others also looked at, then reach into your pocket, leaving the palmed fake behind withdraw the Queen. Now everything can be examined.

A novel publicity effect can be worked with this trick. Instead of a blank card, use an ordinary one but have pasted on it your own advertising matter, such as your

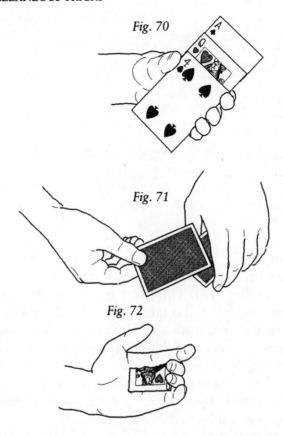

Fig. 70

Fig. 71

Fig. 72

business card or even your photo. At the conclusion of the trick the ad. card can be left with the spectator who will surely keep it as a souvenir and reminder that he saw the trick performed by a first-class conjurer.

JUMPING JOKER

Ten different cards are shown together with the Joker. They are dealt one at a time on the table, each card being turned over as it is dealt. The audience are then able to see that the cards seem to be genuine and that you are not using any sleight of hand.

The Joker is placed on top of the packet which is held

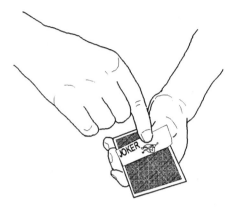

Fig. 73

face down in the left hand. Attention is drawn to the
Joker being on top of the packet by lifting up the top edge
for all to see (Fig. 73). The Joker is pushed off with the
left thumb, the right hand taking it – once more showing
it – placing it second from top. Nothing could be fairer; it
is done quite slowly and deliberately, the cards are tapped
and yet when the top card is bent back it is found to be
the Joker back on top again. Once more it is placed
second from top – another tap and the Joker is thumbed
off the top – yes, it has arrived there again.

It is now openly placed at the bottom of the pack, but
despite this another magic tap is given and the Joker
arrives back on top again. Finally the Joker is placed in
the centre of the packet – the magic tap and the cards are
turned over to reveal the Joker placidly sitting on the
bottom.

Now the cards are counted on to the outstretched hand
of a spectator – and there is only one Joker to be seen.

To the spectators witnessing this trick there seems to be
no other explanation for it, except that you are using very
clever sleight of hand, but everything is done right under
their noses so even this seems to be ruled out.

You use a faked card which is easily made by obtaining
a duplicate Joker and gluing it at one end only to the back
of one of the other cards (Fig. 74).

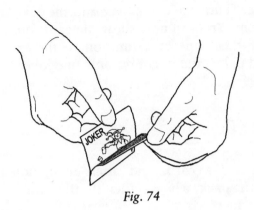

Fig. 74

Besides this fake card you will need about eight or nine others, preferably all the same suit, and of course an unprepared Joker. It is a good idea to place a small pencil dot on the back of the upper edge of the Joker and the fake Joker card so that you know the correct way up.

Have the packet of cards with the genuine Joker on top, the fake card just beneath it second from the top. Turn them over face to the audience and fan them out, count each card separately into the right hand drawing attention to the Joker. Turn them face down and count them again, thus leaving them in their original stack with the Joker on top.

Holding the packet as in Fig. 73, lift up the top edge to reveal the Joker. Now take it off the packet and openly place it second from the top. Give the cards a little flick and cause the Joker to arrive, 'back on top again'. Show the top card as a Joker by turning back the top edge slightly as before. This will be the fake glued Joker, but thumb this off and place it second from the top. Repeat the 'flicking' motion, causing the Joker to jump on top again. Now you can lift it off completely, turning it over so that all can see it. Openly place it on the bottom, flick the cards – turn back the top card – the Joker seems to have arrived back there again.

Finally, place what is apparently the Joker in the centre

of the packet. Turn the cards over and the Joker is seen
on the bottom. You can now show the cards quite freely
by counting them one at a time on to the spectator's
outstretched palm, and of course only one Joker is seen.

TRANSPRINT

Someone selects a card, and after being noted it is
returned to the pack, which is then shuffled and wrapped
in a handkerchief.

The wrapped pack is given to a spectator to hold, and
the performer requests the name of the card. When it is
unwrapped the handkerchief bears the name of the card
selected. The pack is then riffled through and in place of
the selected card there is only a blank one to be seen,
apparently the print has transferred itself to the handkerchief from the card.

This is a highly visual effect and maintains interest
because the audience has something to look at the whole
time.

The method by which the trick is worked is basically
simple. You will require a specially faked handkerchief
bearing the facsimile of a playing card: this is easily made
by laying the handkerchief over a playing card and
tracing the pips onto the fabric using a ball-point pen –
red or black. See Fig. 75.

Fold up the handkerchief so that the picture is con-
cealed (as in Fig. 76), then place it ready in your top
breast pocket. A blank card is put somewhere near the
bottom of the pack and the force card which has been cut
short is on the top. Remove the pack from the case and
ask someone for a number between one and ten. Start
counting the cards into the right hand but finish at the
number called for and replace them back on the pack.
This will leave your force card at the called out number

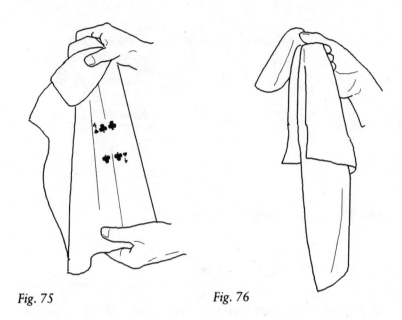

Fig. 75   *Fig. 76*

from the top of the pack. This is apparently by way of indication to the spectator how to count the cards – and you hand them to him requesting that he count his number of cards from the top of the pack noting the card he counted to. This is replaced and the pack shuffled. You meanwhile remove the handkerchief from your pocket, hold it by the top corner allowing it to hang down so that the folds will still conceal the picture. Wrap the pack in the handkerchief and give it to someone to hold. After suitable by-play, get the spectator to unwrap the pack. Everyone sees the card printed on the fabric. You now take the cards and riffle through them: the selected card, being a short one, will not be noticed. Look for the blank card, remove it and pass this and the handkerchief for examination.

If you believe in thoroughly covering up your own tracks, you can take the opportunity to locate the short card and palm it off the pack, then you will be able to let

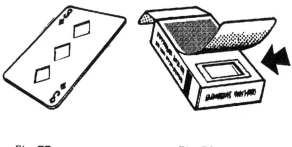

Fig. 77   *Fig. 78*

the spectators examine this as well.

CARD VANISHING CASE

A slightly different version makes use of an ingenious
prop which will cause a card to vanish from the pack.
The effect is much the same plot except that the pack,
which is previously examined, is placed in the card case.
The case is wrapped in the handkerchief as before – and
when unwrapped the cards are tipped out – a 'skeleton'
card makes its appearance. This is a card which has the
pips cut away.

There is no trace of the force card in the pack, which
can again be examined if necessary.

The 'skeleton' pip card is easily made by cutting out all
the pips with a sharp knife. The Three of Diamonds is the
easiest one to prepare. See Fig. 77.

First carefully partly remove the card which is usually
found on the back of the case. With a sharp knife cut a
'window' about an inch square in the back of the case
somewhere near the bottom. Stick a piece of Sellotape
over this cut-out portion so the adhesive side faces in to
the box. Now replace the card on the back of the box,
gluing it in position. See Fig. 78.

When you are ready to present the effect have the

skeleton card on top of the pack, and the force card immediately below it. A gentle pressure on the 'window' will retain the skeleton card in the box when the rest of the cards are tipped out. The top card of the pack will always adhere to the sellotape and stay in the box unknown to the spectators.

The card is forced and returned to the pack – but controlled to the top by means of the pass. As the pack is replaced in the box, pull the blank card forward with the forefinger and insert the cards so that the skeleton goes into the centre. When the cards are finally tipped out of the box at the finish, the top card is retained by means of the stick window and of course the skeleton is found in the centre – the selected card having vanished.

It will readily be seen that the Card Vanishing Case has many practical uses, and the card conjurer will find it quite a useful device.

CARD THROUGH HANDKERCHIEF

For this effect you will need a dark-coloured handkerchief, in the centre of which you place a small dab of wax. A card is selected, returned to the pack, then controlled to the top; you can use the Roly Poly Pass (see page 29) for this move. The pack is placed face down on the table in front of you. Now lay the handkerchief over the cards, diamond fashion, the lower point of the diamond nearest you, the spot of wax just over the centre of the pack (Fig. 79).

Fold over the bottom corner to the centre (Fig. 80), then the left and right corners (Fig. 81), followed by the top corner, but take the opportunity to press down on the wax so that the top card adheres to the underside of the handkerchief (Fig. 82).

As if it's an after-thought, say 'No, that's the wrong way,' and unfold the corners to form a diamond again.

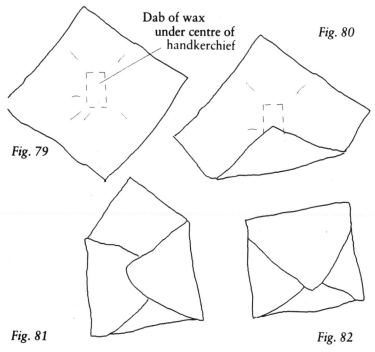

Dab of wax
under centre of
handkerchief

Fig. 80

Fig. 79

Fig. 81

Fig. 82

Pick up the handkerchief between the thumb and fingers of each hand, thumbs on top at a point just above the two corners left and right (Fig. 83). Lift up far enough to allow the top and back corners of the diamond to drop down (Fig. 84). The card will be secretly carried away under the fold of the handkerchief. (The white dotted line indicates card.)

Bring the handkerchief to the front of the pack but with the nearest corner concealing it. Lay it down over the cards again. Fold over the top, left and right corners as before (Figs. 85, 86). Now have someone gently fold the corners back to reveal their selected card staring them in the face having apparently penetrated the handkerchief (Fig. 87).

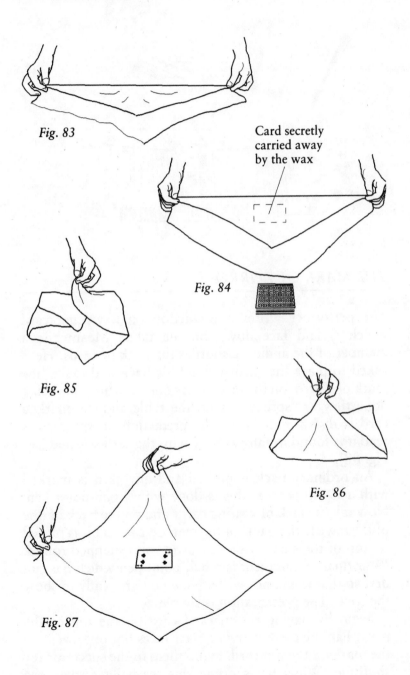

Fig. 83

Card secretly
carried away
by the wax

Fig. 84

Fig. 85

Fig. 86

Fig. 87

Fig. 88

THE MARK OF ZORRO

The performer writes a prediction on a visiting card which is laid face down on the table. Meanwhile a member of the audience shuffles the pack of cards. He is asked to place the cards behind his back and make 'the mark of Zorro' on the face of any one of them. This being done they are spread out on the table and the marked card is discovered. When the prediction on the card is read it is found to tally exactly with the card selected (see Fig. 88).

An ordinary pack is needed and any card is marked with a Z on its face; this is done with a ball-point pen. Now take a stack of visiting cards and on the back of one of them write the name of the marked card. This is placed on top of the stack with an elastic band snapped round. Your final requirement is a ball-point pen which has run dry, so that it will not write. Now you are ready to show the trick. The presentation is simple.

Begin by having the marked card on the top of the pack. Fan the cards showing their faces but not revealing the mark on the top card. Hand them to the spectator for shuffling. While he is doing this, casually display the stack of visiting cards, peel off the top one, holding it writing side to you and pretend to write the prediction. The pen will not write of course, but the name of the card is already written there anyway, so you must go through the motions of actually writing – this is the strong point of the effect.

Now hand the pen to the spectator and have him place this and the cards behind his back and ask him to mark the Z on any card. This he does, and brings forth the pack while you pocket the pen. He has no means of knowing which card was marked.

When they are spread out and the marked card located it will of course be the one that you originally predicted. As a final touch, you could have a duplicate pen in your pocket that really writes – this is identifiable from the other by a nick mark. This you use to turn over the cards to reveal the prediction, and after it is verified make the mark of Zorro on the other side saying, 'Here is a souvenir of the occasion when you made the mark of Zorro.'

CARDS ACROSS MIRACLE

Very rarely does one find a card trick suitable for both parlour and stage presentation, but the Cards Across trick happily falls into these two categories, and what is more, this trick is a real baffler as well as being highly entertaining to the audience. Read what happens.

The performer invites two of the spectators to assist and they are seated on each side of the stage or platform. The table is in the centre and on the table is seen a pack of cards and a packet of envelopes.

The assistant on the right is handed the pack of cards and is instructed to deal ten cards one at a time on to the table. These are placed in an envelope which he seals and keeps safely until the end of the trick.

While he is doing this, the assistant on the left side of the stage is busy counting down another ten cards, after which he is asked to pick them up and go into the audience and have three people each mentally select one of the ten cards. These too are sealed in another envelope which this assistant places in his pocket for safe keeping.

The position is now this: Each assistant has counted and sealed ten cards in an envelope which he retains in his possession. One of the assistants, however, has had three of his ten cards specially noted. It seems unlikely that any trickery can be effected with this situation. nevertheless the magician now causes three cards to vanish from one envelope, in spite of the fact that it has been held securely by the assistant, and to magically appear in the other envelope which has been in the safe keeping of the second assistant. Not only do the cards pass across, but amazing as it may seem, they are the actual mentally selected cards. The cards and envelopes are passed out for complete inspection.

I know that this particular effect sounds like a miracle and indeed it looks like it too, because the performer is definitely unaware of the cards chosen, yet these are the very ones that arrive in the envelope.

However, read on for the secret.

Preparation: You will need two packs of cards and a packet of ordinary envelopes. From the first pack remove any ten assorted cards, and from the other remove exactly the same ten duplicates. Now from the first pack take out the ten corresponding cards in value, but different suit of the same colour. For instance, if you remove the Jack of Clubs, then you need a Jack of Clubs from the other pack, and the Jack of Spades from the original pack.

Although any combination of cards will do, in order to keep things clear, I suggest the following as a suitable selection. From the:

Have the cards from the first pack in any order face down, and under these place the duplicate cards from the

First Pack: 3♡ 8♠ 8◇ 2♣ 6◇ K◇ 9◇ A♡ 7♠ J♣
Second Pack: 3♡ 8♠ 8◇ 2♣ 6◇ K◇ 9◇ A♡ 7♠ J♣
First Pack: 3◇ 8♣ 8♡ 2♠ 6♡ K♡ 9♡ A◇ 7♣ J♠

second pack, in any order, also face down, and beneath these the balance of the first pack in any order face down. Place them ready in the card case.

Now take any three of the remaining ten cards from the first pack and place them face down between the flap of the top envelope and finally place the last seven cards inside the bottom envelope. Put the original maker's band around the packet or secure with an elastic band. Then put the prepared full pack of cards under the band and you are all ready to perform.

The remainder of the cards from pack No. 2 can now be discarded as they are not required for the trick.

Presentation: Request the assistance of two helpers and seat them either side of the table.

Remove the cards from the case and false shuffle, leaving the order undisturbed.

Hand the cards to the right-hand assistant, ask him to count the cards one at a time face downwards on to the table, counting aloud for all to hear.

While he is doing this, pick up the packet of envelopes and rip off the band, take the envelope (the one with the three cards under the flap), replacing the remainder on the table.

Without exposing the three cards, wait until the assistant has finished counting then drop the envelope (and also, secretly, the three cards) on to his counted pile.

Take the balance of the cards from him and hand them to the left-hand assistant.

Pick up the envelope and hold it open, then gesture to the right-hand assistant to pick up the cards and drop them in. When he has done this, immediately hand it to him to seal and then ask him to sit down. You have, of course, neatly added three cards to his ten. Now ask the left-hand assistant to count out ten cards face down on to the table, and when he has done this, have him go among the audience and get three people to mentally select a card. Ask him to be sure that the three cards selected are all different.

Having done this, the cards are brought back and placed in the empty envelope on top. Gesture to him to sit down, and in doing so turn the packet over, bringing the envelope containing seven cards to the top. In the same movement slide this forward for him to take, which he seals and puts straight into his pocket.

This turnover move is accomplished by ample misdirection at the critical moment, and is covered by the attention drawn to the spectator being asked to sit down. Dispose of the remainder of the envelopes in your pocket, and the trick is now done as far as you are concerned.

In pantomime, cause three cards to transfer themselves from the left-hand assistant to those held by the man on the right. Then the man on the left opens his envelope and counts them aloud to find there are only seven. The three members of the audience who selected the cards then call them out. They are the three cards found to be missing from the ten.

The man on the right now opens his envelope and finds thirteen, and among them you have the three cards selected. There you have it, the famous Cards Across Miracle. There is no real sleight-of-hand involved, except perhaps for the false shuffle and even that can be omitted, but to make things complete, the false shuffle will be found described in Chapter Two, page 33

One more word, because this trick is based on simple subterfuges it is even more important to heighten the effect by good showmanship. Check your card set-up before you present the effect and you will find that there is a no more baffling trick with which you can mystify an audience.

It has been found that the same effect can be worked

Fig. 89

using Jumbo cards (giant-sized cards), thus a really super stage effect can be added to your repertoire.

FLIP FLAP

It is surprising how some people's power of observation can play tricks on them. This is a card trick which cleverly makes use of that failing. 'Here is a black nine and a black ten,' says the performer, and openly puts them in different parts of the pack which is fanned out face upwards so that everyone can see them. The pack is now rolled in a handkerchief. A spectator unwraps the pack, but to everyone's surprise the two cards are seen to have come together in the pack – and what is more they are found reversed.

Take a look at the illustration (Fig. 89). Which cards are in the left hand – the Ten of Spades and the Nine of Clubs, or is it the Nine of Clubs and the Ten of spades? Unless you take a second look, it isn't easy to remember, is it?

Remove each of these four cards from the pack to begin with, then place a Nine and a Ten together but reversed near the top of the pack, the other Nine and Ten are put near each other, but facing the proper way towards the bottom of the deck.

With the cards thus set up in their case you are all ready to work the effect.

Remove the pack and fan them face towards you, but do not include the top part of the pack in the fan. Sort through the fan removing the Ten and the Nine previously placed there. Draw attention to these saying, 'Here is the black Nine and the black Ten.' Put one near the top and one near the bottom of the pack.

Close the fan and have someone cut it, completing the cut. Fold a handkerchief into a strip, wrapping it around the pack. Ask someone to give it a tap, then unroll the cards. On looking through the pack two cards will be found reversed, and they will appear to be those just put in haphazardly a few moments ago.

It will readily be seen that the business of wrapping the cards in a handkerchief is just a piece of 'padding' designed to put the spectators off the scent. There are not many people who will realize that the two cards first shown are not in fact exactly the same as the ones eventually found reversed in the pack.

CHAPTER SIX

Guest Artists

O N Monday nights the Magic Circle, at its temporary headquarters in London, is thronged with
magicians amateur and professional, many of them from
distant parts of the world. They can be seen gathered
together in little groups discussing and showing one
another the latest sleights and tricks. It would not have
been improbable to find all of our guest contributors
engaged in such a manner, even though they were from
different quarters of the world. Their interest in magic
was similar.

There is always something new to be seen – some new
'move', or a different way to do an old trick, making this
hobby of magic so fascinating. That is why I have asked
each of them to contribute something for our final
chapter.

'Make it an easy trick,' I said. 'Give our reader
something that you yourself have enjoyed doing,' which
they did quite readily in just the same spirit that can be
found among magicians everywhere; because it cannot be
denied that wherever you go, whether it be in the
hallowed 'Circle' clubroom, back-stage with a professional, in the private home of an experienced amateur or
with an enthusiastic beginner – you will discover that
they have all been fired with that love of doing magic and
showing tricks: the Americans call it the magic 'bug'. I
hope by now that you have also developed that enthusi-

asm, and have been well and truly bitten by that magic 'bug'.

FRANK CURLEY

Frank Curley in public life was really a statistician with the London County Council, and his facile mathematical brain was often brought to bear on the many card tricks he has devised.

Of course inventing and performing card tricks was his spare time activity.

I am most pleased to include the following trick in this book, because it makes use of the Curley Force, which he invented. He first described it to me during the war and I have made great use of it ever since.

THE ATOMIC CARD TRICK

Effect: Two cards chosen by spectators are returned to the pack, which is shuffled and cut by a member of the audience. The magician puts the pack into his trousers pocket and withdraws one card, which is one of the two selected previously. On removing the remainder of the pack from his pocket, he puts the single card on top of the pack and places the complete pack into a glass tumbler, the face of the pack being towards the audience. After covering the tumbler with a handkerchief, the second spectator is asked to think of his chosen card, then to imagine it breaking up into atoms and reassembling at the face of the pack as a complete card. The handkerchief is removed and the face card is seen to be the second chosen card and the spectator is congratulated on his powers of imagination.

Requirements: One pack of cards, one double-faced

card, a method forcing two cards, a tumbler and a handkerchief.

Method: Two cards are forced, returned to the pack, which is shuffled and cut. The magician then puts the pack into his right trousers pocket, where he has the double-faced card. As the forced cards match the faces of the fake card, when the fake card is taken from the pocket it appears to be one of the chosen cards. Removing the pack, the magician adds the fake to the top, so that the second face is uppermost facing himself. The pack must be held with its normal face card towards the audience; the pack is put in a tumbler and in covering with the handkerchief the tumbler is given a half turn, thereby bringing the face of the fake card towards the audience. Thus when the covering is removed the second chosen card seems to be at the face of the pack.

Double-faced card: This is simply two playing cards stuck together back to back, although it is possible nowadays to obtain double-faced and double-backed cards from magical dealers.

CURLEY'S CARD FORCE

This can be used to force one or more cards, and they should be in position on top of the pack.

The action used is similar to that usually used when looking through a pack to find a certain card; the pack is passed a few cards at a time, face up, from the left to the right hand.

To force a card, however, the pack is held in the left hand at chest level, the pack vertical but with the faces to the audience. Passing the cards slowly across from the left to right hand the magician asks a spectator to say 'Stop' whenever he wishes. Masked by the spread of the cards, the right thumb pushes the top card to the left (Fig. 90) and at the moment when the spectator says 'Stop' the

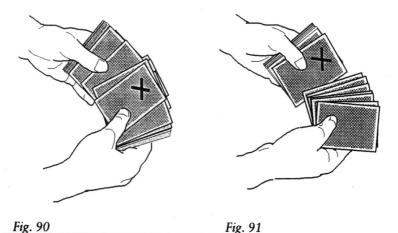

Fig. 90   *Fig. 91*

magician separates the cards in his right hand from those in the left, but leaves the original top card on top of the left-hand packet. This is held out to the spectator to remember (Fig. 91).

The pack is squared up and the action is repeated with the second spectator, forcing the new top card, which was the original second card in the pack.

LEN MASON

Len Mason was a successful Australian business man, though actually he went there from England in 1920 after serving in the First World War. A member of the Inner Magic Circle (Gold Star) and past president of the Sydney Ring of the International Brotherhood of Magicians, he had been interested in magic for over fifty years and he told me that he still enjoyed doing card tricks best of all – in fact he gained quite a reputation as a 'card man'. He followed magic purely as a hobby, but found it enormously advantageous during the course of business, Len was one of those rare fellows who could combine business with pleasure. In fact the trick which follows was done at a business luncheon one day – no cards being available, he carried right on and did a card trick nevertheless.

CARD TRICK WITHOUT CARDS

When called upon to do a trick say, 'I'd be pleased to but I have nothing with me, but if we can all pretend that I have a pack of cards I would like to do a card trick for you.' Pretend to shuffle the imaginary pack, dropping one (apparently), then picking it up, saying, 'Ah, the Seven of Spades, my favourite card.'

Approach a spectator with a request for him to think of any card he can see. Of course he can see nothing, but you say 'This is all pretence, just think of your favourite card – any card – not the Joker because I will take this out.' Pretend to look for the Joker and place it in your pocket. 'Right – you have your card in mind.' Do this to two, three or four people. 'Now comes the difficult part – for me, not you, because I just want you to multiply the value of your card by ten – Jack is counted as eleven, Queen is twelve and the King is thirteen. The easiest way to multiply by ten is just to add a nought – nowt difficult in that! Now add, say, eight to the total. Then if it is a Club add one, if a Heart add two, if Spades add three and add four if it is a Diamond. Done that? Now what is your total?'

A spectator gives it and you then silently subtract eight from the total immediately you know the card. Do this with each spectator.

The secret is so simple and yet so good that although you do this for many spectators, they will not discover the method.

I give two examples which will explain this quite well. Suppose the first spectator thinks of the Four of Clubs; multiply by ten which gives you forty, then add eight, making forty-eight, and then one for the value of Clubs, making forty-nine in all. When they give you the total, deduct the number which you gave them to add, which in this case was eight, and you get forty-one – Four of Clubs – because you already know that Clubs are valued at one.

If the King of Diamonds is thought of, the King is thirteen, multiplied by ten makes 130, add eight making 138, then add four for the value of Diamonds, a total of 142. Deduct eight, this gives you 134. Thirteen is a King and four a Diamond.

Don't pass this because it is easy and simple to do. I have done this for years and nobody has said 'Oh I know how that is done.' You need not always add eight – any number will do so long as you deduct that number from the total. When they give you their total you get the thought-of-card 'on a plate'.

Hope you like this and have as much fun as I have had, and will continue to have as long as I can get two or three gathered together to put up with me.

THE GREAT MASONI

The Great Masoni was a member of the famous Inner Magic Circle and a successful illusionist. He was equally at home performing before cabaret audiences, showing intimate magic, as well as on the stage, on television and in films, presenting such fabulous illusions as Sawing through a Woman. He toured the world with his stage illusion show 'Out of the Hat'.

He presented his charming wife Shan in an amazing demonstration of a feat of memory. You will have seen him in the film with James Mason, *Passport to Pimlico*, on theatre stages everywhere and of course very frequently on television. Now work one of his card tricks that he has used to baffle those audiences.

DO AS I DO

The trick I will now explain is original to me only as far as the routine is concerned. It is the combination of the two oldest principles of card magic, a very easy card control, and 'The Conjurer's Choice'. Although this is one of the easiest card tricks I know, its effect on a lay audience is always excellent. I include it in all my cabaret engagements, which are made up mostly of sophisticated all-male private parties at such places as The Dorchester and Mayfair Hotels in London. Let the beginner bear in mind that the audience is only interested in the *effect*, not the method by which it is brought about. So do not discard this because of its simplicity for with good showmanship it is an absolute winner.

Effect: The performer explains that anyone can do a card trick provided he does exactly as the performer. A volunteer selects a card, it is returned to the pack and shuffled. Although he has no idea where his card is, he discovers it successfully by following the same moves as the performer under his instructions.

Method: Have a card selected from the pack and remembered. As you extend the pack for him to return his card, cut the pack with the right hand, and as you put forward your left hand for him to replace the card, very slightly tip the pack in your right hand towards yourself and get a glance of the bottom card of the pack – we will call this the key card.

Don't do it too obviously. You will find that if you keep your right hand a little higher than the left, the 'tip' and the 'glance' will not be noticed.

When the helper has replaced his card on the top of the packet in the left hand, drop the right-hand packet slowly and deliberately on the left-hand packet, pointing out the fact that the card is completely lost in the pack. Pretend to hear someone doubt it. Turn the pack over and say to

the helper, 'Look and see that your card is still in the
centre of the pack, but don't tell me when you see it.' Run
through the pack and watch for the key card – when you
see it, run on for about two or three cards further, stop,
and ask helper if he saw his card. As you speak to him,
cut the pack at the spot you stopped at, and turn the pack
over. This brings the chosen card three or four from the
top. Say to the helper, 'See – your card is nowhere near
the top,' (as you are saying this, pick up and turn over
one card after the other from the top until you come to
the key card). Place the cards you have taken off (including the key card) into the pack – turn over the pack and
continue, 'And nowhere near the bottom,' showing a few
cards in the same manner from the bottom and putting
them in the pack. The chosen card is now on top of the
pack.

If you like, you can give the following false shuffle. Cut
the pack and interleave the two halves end-to-end with
both hands, just as most card players do, but see that the
half on which is the chosen card is larger than the other
and when interleaving see that a few cards and the chosen
card remain on top of the pack.

Place the pack on the table then ask the helper to cut
the pack into two halves. Ask him to choose whichever
packet he likes. Tell him to pick it up, and you pick up the
other. Remember whether he picked the packet containing the chosen card or whether you are left with it. (You
can forget, I did once but I took a chance and I was right
more by luck.)

Tell him to do exactly as you do, deal one card on the
table in front of you. The helper does the same in front of
him. You deal another on the left of your card on the
table, the helper does the same. You deal another card on
the right – the helper does the same. You now have two
sets of three cards, one set in front of you, and the other
in front of the helper.

Ask the helper to indicate any set of three he likes. If he

chooses the one containing the chosen card, pick up your set and return it to the pack. If he indicates your set, pick it up and return it to the pack. So whichever way, the set with the chosen card is left on the table.

Note: Use the word 'indicate' not 'select' as the former can be translated either way to your advantage.

Now ask the helper to indicate one of the remaining three cards. If he points to the centre card (make the most of it, ask him if he wants to change his mind), pick up the other two cards, return them to the pack. Ask him the name of the card he chose. When he names it, dramatically have him turn it over. If he points to one of the *end* ones, ask him to point to another ('Point' is also another good ambiguous word.) If he points to the other end one, draw attention to the fact that he has had a free choice and he can change his mind. Return them to the pack, and disclose the remaining card as above.

If he points to the chosen card the second time tell the helper to keep his fingers on both of them. Take away the remaining card and return it to the pack. Ask the helper to lift his finger from one of the two. If he lifts his finger from the chosen card, say, 'That's the one you want?' at the same time picking up the other card from under his finger and returning it to the pack. If he lifts his finger from the other card, return it to the pack and continue as above to disclose the card.

I think with due modesty that this way of using the 'conjurer's choice' is the most unsuspicious. The old way of using the words 'choose' and 'select' and then remarking, to suit your purpose, 'Then that leaves me this one,' is to me very suspicious. The above allows your actions to be interpreted as you wish without any suspicion.

Anyway I haven't had anyone spot it. Do try it.

Note: Work this effect very deliberately – pointing out over and over again that the helper has an absolute free choice, and can change his mind at any time. This amplifies the denouement at the end, and adds to the mystery.

REG SALMON

Reg Salmon achieved fame over the years as a stage illusionist, having appeared on the principal music hall stages and on television, presenting his super-size mysteries; but he also specialised in close-up magic and intimate card tricks.

Those who knew him will have seen him work the following trick and although basically simple in method, is one of the best of all close-up impromptu tricks with cards.

ALL CHANGE

This is a 'Follow my Leader' effect using ten cards.

Begin by openly removing five red cards and five black cards from the pack – the rest of which is discarded.

Show them spread out in a fan as in Fig. 92. The red cards are on top, the black ones beneath. The left thumb rests on the fourth black card from the left. The tips of the right fingers rest against the back of the fifth black card. This is a perfectly natural hold and you will probably find that your fingers will automatically position themselves at these points without much manoeuvring. Now comes the only really fake move in the routine. You appear to separate the two sets of cards; black cards are closed into the left hand, the red ones into the right. But the fifth or top black card is secretly added to the bottom of the red stack, the right finger-tips assisting. The red set is placed face up on the table and you say, 'Here are five red cards.' The black cards are

Fig. 92

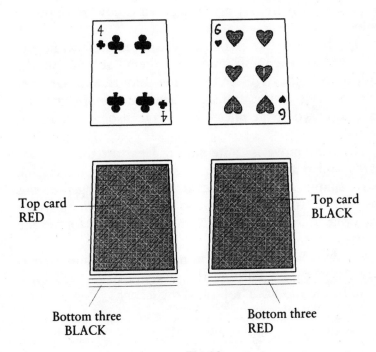

Top card
RED

Top card
BLACK

Bottom three
BLACK

Bottom three
RED

Fig. 93

placed face up on top of the reds: 'And here are the five blacks.'

Pick all the cards up in the left hand and turn them face down as if for dealing. Now count off the top five cards keeping them in the same order. Square them up and turn them face up on the table saying, 'Five red cards.' Count the remaining five, being careful to keep them in the same order and face down while you count. Square them up laying them face up by the side of the others saying, 'And here the five black.'

Pick off the top red card, placing it just in front of the same stack. Do the same with the top black card. Now turn the stacks face down. The audience will merely think that you have two stacks of cards, one red and the other black, each indicated by the same colour leader card.

In actual fact the position is as in Fig. 93. The top card of each pile when they are face down is now an opposite colour.

Openly change over the indicator cards. Turn up the top card of each pile and deal them face up on the indicators – they will be the same colours. Change over the positions of the indicator cards once more, turn up each top card of the piles – they have also changed their colour.

The next move is quite subtle. Deal off the top two cards and place them face down over their indicators. Now change over the indicator piles including the ones just put on top. Turn up these top face-down cards on each pile – they have also changed colour to follow the leader.

Finally, change the positions of the remaining two face-down cards. Turning them face up they will once more be seen to have 'followed the leader'.

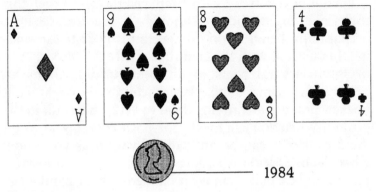

Fig. 94

JOE STUTHARD

Joe Stuthard, although Canadian, can be called a veritable international performer. With his wife Kay he has toured the world many times showing his magic in theatre, cabaret and on television everywhere.

Best-known for his fabulous feats with a pack of cards, he is also an inventor of card tricks. His act makes use of extreme dexterity on the one hand and sweet simplicity on the other. The trick which follows is in the latter category but has that strong effective finish so apparent in all Joe's presentations.

UP-TO-DATE CARDS

Joe asks for the loan of any coin. This is placed tail side downwards in a prominent position on the table. Now someone takes a pack of cards and deals them into two piles. One of these is selected. The top four cards of this pile are dealt face down in a row and the rest of the pack is discarded.

For the first time the date on the coin is looked at and the cards now slowly turned over – they are seen to tally exactly with the date (see Fig. 94).

Do not be deterred by the simple method by which this trick is brought about. Although it requires so little preparation the effect on the spectators is quite astounding. Let us deal with the coin first of all.

Obtain several coins of different denominations all bearing the same date, place them in the right coat pocket, practise identifying them by feel whilst still in the pocket. When you ask for the loan of a coin, lay stress on the fact that it can be any coin. As soon as you know what denomination it is, locate the similar coin in your pocket and casually remove it palmed in your hand. (The word 'palmed' is used loosely here, for actually you need only have the coin in your hand held against the palm with the closed fingers and no special practice is required because it is a perfectly natural hold.)

With this hand take the borrowed coin and place it in your other hand, which immediately lays it date side down on the table. Actually what happens is that you effect a 'switch' of coins. Remember the audience do not know what you are going to do at this stage and have no reason to suspect anything untoward.

As you take the borrowed coin between your fingers and thumb, keep a firm grasp on it, but allow the palmed one to fall into your hand. Let the borrowed coin take the palmed position formerly held by the other coin. But do not hesitate here, keep everyone's attention on your left hand which openly places the coin on the table. Tell everyone you will put the coin date side down and to keep their eyes on it.

Reach into your pocket with the right hand, leave the borrowed coin behind and bring out a pack of cards. The cards were previously prepared by sorting out the four cards which will represent the date and placing them alternately with four other cards on the bottom of the pack.

The rest is easy. After removing the cards from your pocket put them on the table asking a spectator to remove them from the case and to deal them into two

piles. The four special cards will all fall together on one of
the piles. Note which one it is, and ask for one pile to be
selected. If the correct pile is chosen, get your assistant to
deal the top four cards face down in a row on the table. If
the other half is chosen get him to cut it into four equal
piles, then deal one card on top of each pile for the
remaining half. When these four are turned over they will
of course indicate the date on the 'borrowed' coin.

Don't forget to return it to the lender.

PHIL WYE

Phil Wye knew the author for well over twenty-five years,
and was an active performer for nearly forty years. He
sold and demonstrated magic in several London stores.
His magical lectures and demonstrations were seen by
several different Magical Clubs, and he showed his
close-up magic at the Magic Circle 'At-Homes'.

COINCIDENCE OR MAGIC?

AS the audience see it . . .

A wallet or envelope is placed on the table and the
magician states that it contains a prediction of events to
come.

A card is now chosen from, say, a red-backed pack. It
is for example the Two of Hearts. It is now placed face up
in the centre of the red pack which has been spread face
down on the table.

The prediction is now taken from the envelope or
wallet and is seen to be a playing card, another Two of
Hearts. The performer states that this could be a coincidence.

He then snaps his fingers over both the face-up cards,
and says 'if that's a coincidence, this could be magic . . .'

The card in the red pack is now shown to have a blue back, and the prediction card to have a red back – the backs have apparently changed places.

How it's done . . .

First place a blue-backed card face down on the bottom of the red pack. A like card (say a Two of Hearts) is placed face up in an envelope or wallet, and this is placed on the table in full view of the audience. Now take the red pack in the right hand, and using the Hindu or Pull-through shuffle (see page 33) force the Two of Hearts. Turn the top portion of the pack face up after the selection and slide the chosen card face up on the table. Spread the pack face down, then insert the face-up card in the centre of the spread pack.

Take out and show the prediction card, keeping it face up whilst speaking about the coincidence.

Snap fingers over both cards, turning them over to reveal the apparent change of backs as described above.

HUBERT CADDY

One of the interesting facets of magic as a hobby is that it draws enthusiasts from all walks of life, all trades and professions. Hubert Caddy, for instance, was a successful architect and an equally successful conjurer, and could be truly termed an all-round magical performer. As well as being in demand as a slick cabaret artiste he was also a great children's entertainer. Some time ago, just before these words were written, the author had the pleasure of introducing Hubert to a large audience of Continental magicians in Amsterdam where he performed his skilful card manipulations, and was received with much acclaim.

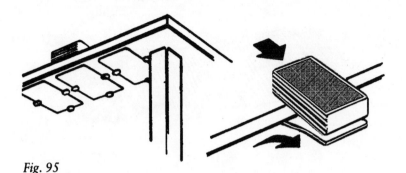

Fig. 95

BAKER'S DOZEN

Twelve cards are counted down onto the table, but every time they are checked they are found to be thirteen in spite of the odd card being discarded every time.

A plain table is used but under its edge are a series of three drawing pins (thumb-tacks) positioned as in the sketch (Fig. 95). Two are placed one inch from the edge of the table, the width of a card apart, and the other in the centre of these just over a card's length from the edge.

In these rest two cards. Prepare four or five groups in this fashion.

The cards are counted down onto the table. Gather them up into a rough pile drawing them off the back edge of the table into the left hand. As you do this the left fingers reach beneath the table and withdraws the two hidden cards and they are secretly added to the pile.

They are counted slowly down onto the table, but the last two are held together and counted as one. The spectators see you count thirteen. You openly discard one and count once more, a genuine count this time. You still have thirteen. You throw the odd one away. Gather them up as before. This time you secretly add the extra two, repeating the moves until your hidden caches of cards are used up.

As a finale you could add say ten cards instead of two,

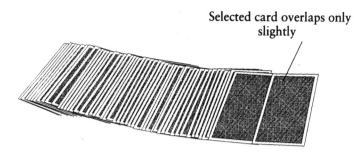

Fig. 96

handing them to someone to count, causing quite a bit of fun as each extra card is counted.

SNAP REVERSE

A great number of card tricks consist of having a card chosen and then finding it somewhere, somehow. In this trick the card is found reversed in the pack, and if performed briskly it will make quite a nice interlude when performing a series of other card effects.

The card is selected, noted and returned to the pack, and then secretly brought to the top by means of the Pass (see page 27). Or if you wish, you can keep a break above the card, then lift all those above the break, shuffling them to the bottom of the pack and keeping the faces towards the audience as you do so. The selected card is on top of the pack, so turn the pack face down and ribbon spread them from left to right (see page 48). Turn the cards over, asking them if they can see their card. They will not see it because during the turnover the tricky move took place. When you originally spread the cards face down the top card (selected) will be at the extreme right-hand end and this is casually pushed well over so that only its left edge overlaps the preceding card, whereas all the others overlap all but ⅛ inch or ¼ inch. See Fig. 96.

When the turnover move is carried out each card turns its neighbour over except the last one which stays face down. You can assist here by lightly resting the tip of the right forefinger on this card, to prevent it turning over accidentally. Now gather up the cards, cut them, complete the cut bringing the now reversed card to the centre. Ribbon spread them once more and the selected card will be seen reversed in the centre of the spread.

Glossary

*A*LMOST every sport, hobby and technical subject seems to develop its own peculiar set of words which are not in everyday usage. Perhaps there are some in this book which may cause a little mystification to the beginner, so a short glossary has been compiled. This follows now, together with other information which the reader might find useful.

Aquitment A series of moves, or a manoeuvre, during the presentation of an effect, mostly applicable to sleight of hand, move usually to make something vanish or keep it hidden.

Backpalm To conceal a card or object at the back of the hand. (See also **Palm**).

Backs The back or pattern side of playing cards, conversely the sides which depict the values are the **Faces**.

Bottom Card Refers to the bottom card or face of the pack, or that which can be seen when the pack is assembled. Opposite to **Top Card** which designates the topmost card of the pack.

Bottom Deal To deal the bottom card of the pack secretly, instead of the top.

Bottom Stock The portion of the pack which is at the bottom.

Break A gap held by the tip of the finger in a particular place in a pack of cards.

Bridge A gap or separation in a pack made by bending some of the cards.

British Ring An influential British Magical Society boasting a very considerable membership. They hold a gigantic

Convention each year which is attended by visiting magicians from all parts of the globe. (See **I.B.M.**)

Conjurer's Choice A spectator's choice or selection which, although ostensibly a free one, is in fact determined by the conjurer.

Crimp To bend secretly one of the corners of a card.

Cull To secretly assemble together, or to extract a number of cards.

Cut 'To cut the pack' is to divide the cards; 'to complete the cut' is to remove a quantity of cards from the top of the pack and place them on the bottom.

Deck A pack of cards. Term common in U.S.A. – but it is also the old English name for a pack.

Ditch To dispose of secretly, to leave behind.

Double Lift The act of lifting two cards together and holding them to appear as one card. **Triple Lift** with three cards and so on (see page 32).

Double-faced Card Made by sticking two cards back to back, similarly with a **Double Back** so that a back design shows on both sides, but specially printed cards of this type are now available at the Magic dealers (see also page 55).

Effect The general impression which the trick makes on the audience or what it looks like to the spectator.

Fair Shuffle As opposed to **False Shuffle**, the cards are genuinely mixed.

Fake or Feke (seen or unseen) See also **Gimmick**. The part of the apparatus which is prepared in such a way as to make possible the result of the trick. To be **Faked** denotes that the apparatus, although it seems to be ordinary, has been secretly altered to create the desired effect.

False Cut To apparently cut the cards – yet leaving it in its previous order.

False Shuffle The cards are mixed (**Shuffled**) in a seemingly innocent way but actually the order of the pack remains undisturbed. Sometimes the pack could be subjected to a genuine shuffle and yet the top stock remain under the performer's control: this would still be termed a **False Shuffle** (see pages 33 and 35).

Fan The best means of exhibiting cards is to spread them fanwise. A few cards or a whole pack, usually employed when offering the cards for one to be selected. **Card Fanning** (not dealt with in this book) is the exhibition of fancy fans, most pretty to watch.

First Card The first card dealt whether the pack is held face down or face up. Or the top card of the pack when held face down.

First Finger (Forefinger) (Index finger) Denotes finger next to the thumb. The others are designated, 2nd, 3rd and 4th – the 4th being the little finger.

Flourish A movement which is done openly, usually to display dexterity such as executing a neat fan, spread or fancy shuffle. But **Flourishes** also serve a useful purpose in that they provide **Misdirection** whilst some other secret move is made.

Force To 'force a card' is to make a spectator select a card you wish him to take although he believes it to be a free choice.

Forefinger See above.

Free Selection Signifies that the spectator has been given a wholly free choice; his selection, not having been influenced by the conjurer.

Gimmick Conjurers have used this word for years, but now it seems to have crept into common usage. In the magical sense, however, it is a piece of apparatus used by the conjurer the presence of which is unknown to the audience (see also **Feke**; e.g. if we stick two cards together or make one short, we say the card has been **Gimmicked**.

Glide Basically used to substitute one card for another, the originally shown card being slid back so the next one is taken (see page 45).

Glimpse or **Peek** To catch a secret glance at, and taking note of a card, also known as **Sighting** a card.

Hindu Shuffle Can be used as genuine shuffle but also as a means of controlling one or a complete stock of cards. (See **Pull Through Shuffle**, page 33).

I.B.M. The **International Brotherhood of Magicians**. An International magical organization with its foundations in America. Divided into 'Rings', many in the U.S.A. and in most other countries. The **British Ring** is No. 25 which incidentally is the largest.

Index Finger See **First Finger**.

Indifferent Card Denotes card other than that designated in the experiment at the time, i.e. the four Aces are specific cards – all others are indifferent. Or a card other than those with which the trick is being performed.

Injog To replace a card back in the pack so that its end projects towards the conjurer.

Inner Magic Circle See **Magic Circle**.

Jog To replace a card so that its end projects slightly – see also **Outjog**.

Key Card A predetermined card which will assist in the location of another. Could also be a **Locator** or **Short Card** or even a **Glimpsed Card**.

Locate To find a card or establish control of its position in the pack.

Locator As in **Key Card**, but to locate means to find a card or establish and control its position in the pack.

London Society of Magicians A lively and distinguished Magic Club with headquarters in London. Its members maintain a high standard of performance.

Long Card A playing card slightly longer than the rest (see also **Short Card**). This enables it to be easily located.

Magic Circle Probably the best known of all the magical societies, it has a very large membership drawn from all parts of the world. Until its recent move to temporary premises, it was proud of its own spacious clubroom in London which also housed one of the finest magical libraries ever collected. Soon, again there will be an impressive magical museum, and a small Theatre. The **Inner Magic Circle** is composed of members who have excelled themselves in magic.

Misdirection To divert the attention of the spectators whilst some secret move or sleight takes place. (See

Flourish.)

Move The manoeuvre which is executed by the conjurer to bring about the trick, e.g. to 'pass' a card to the top.

Nail Nick To mark a card secretly by pressing it with the thumb or finger-nail so as to identify it later.

One-way Pack A pack with a non-reversible back – an obvious example would be a design incorporating say a picture of a dog. If one card in the pack is reversed, the dog would be seen upside down and then the card is easily picked out from the rest. But of course it is better to use a pack with a reverse design not so easily detected.

Operator Name given to a performer. Usually applicable to sleight of hand.

Outjog To replace a card in the pack so the edge projects away from the performer. (See also **Injog.**)

Overhand Shuffle A genuine shuffle, the one most generally used by card players; but the top stack of cards can be retained and controlled by using a **False Overhand Shuffle.**

Pack A pack of cards – modern pack consists usually of 52 plus 2 Jokers. Some Continental packs have 32 cards. (See **Deck.**)

Palm To secretly conceal some small object in the hand.

Pass This is dealt with extensively in Chapter 2.

Peek See **Glimpse.**

Pre-arrangement The beforehand arrangement of the pack in set order. (See **Set Up.**)

Prepare The faking of the pack – to arrange it ready for the performance. 'The pack is prepared as follows:–'

Principle The basic method by which the trick is accomplished.

Readers Cards which have secret marks on the backs so that their values can be 'read' without seeing the faces.

Reversed Card A card which is returned to the pack upside down or back to front.

Riffle The cards are held in the left hand as if for dealing, the second finger of the right hand bends the top edges upwards allowing them to fall consecutively.

Routine The arrangement or running order of a group of tricks or when applicable to one trick refers to the sequence of moves made in order to present it effectively.

Second Deal Where the second card, instead of the first card, is dealt from the pack. Not an easy sleight to perform. (See also **Bottom Deal.**)

Set Up The pre-arrangement of the pack in a certain order.

Short Card One that is a trifle shorter, used as a **Key Card** etc. A **Long Card** can be used in the same way. Similar are **wide** and **narrow** cards.

Showmanship The very essence of presentation. Showmanship highlights the difference between a mediocre performance and an outstanding one. Some people have a natural flair for it, but it can also be achieved with experience.

Shuffle To mix the cards.

Sight As in **Glimpse** or **Peek.**

Sleights Manoeuvres performed by the conjurer to accomplish a desired effect. **Sleight of Hand** as applied to **Sleights** or **Moves,** usually secretly by using the hands but distinct from **Flourishes** because **Sleights** should be invisible or at least be unsuspected by the audience.

Slick Card A highly polished card which slides easier than the rest – used as a Locator.

Spread Sometimes **Ribbon Spread,** the cards being spread on the table in a row (see page 48).

Square Up After the cards have been dealt, counted or shuffled they are then formed into a neat stack again.

Stack A pre-arranged pack of cards.

Steal To secretly secure a card unknown to the audience.

Stock A group of cards that you may wish to keep control of; e.g., if the top 'stock' were in a set order you could false shuffle but still retain this 'stock' in the same position.

Strippers Cards which have been tapered so they are wider at one end than the other. When one is reversed it is easily 'stripped' out. Also called a **Biseaute** pack.

Switch To exchange one object secretly for another, e.g. one card for another, or a faked pack for a genuine one.

Table Trick An effect suitable mainly for an audience grouped or sitting round a table.

Thick Card Made by sticking two cards together and used as a locator or key card (see also **Short Card**). A make-shift **Thick Card** can be temporarily made by moistening the back of any card and allowing the Joker to adhere to it. A variation of the **Thick Card** can be made by cutting a panel around the design of a card and sticking it to the back of another so the design matches exactly.

Throw To deposit the balance of the cards on to the pack after a shuffle.

Thumb Count To secretly count the cards whilst held in one hand, using the thumb.

Top Card See **Bottom Card**.

Top Stock The upper part of the pack when it is held face down – see **Bottom Stock**.

Transposition A basic effect in magic: one article is magically caused to change places with another.

Undercut To take the lower section of the pack and replace it on the upper section.

ppercut The obverse of the **Undercut**, i.e. to take the upper section and place it beneath the lower section of the pack.

Vanish Another basic effect, what it implies to cause any object to disappear.

Wax Sometimes called **Conjurer's Wax**. Used to cause one card to adhere to the other.